Pelican Books
Caught in the Act

Marcel Berlins was b
educated mainly in S
degrees in commerce and law at the University of the Witwatersrand. After a short period in practice as a solicitor he left South Africa to study international law in Paris, and then came to England, where he obtained a Master of Laws degree at the London School of Economics. He is now legal correspondent of *The Times* and lives in London.

Geoffrey Wansell was born in Scotland in 1945 and was brought up in London, where he still lives. He graduated from the London School of Economics in 1966 and, after flirting briefly with academic life, joined *The Times Educational Supplement* in 1967 as a trainee reporter. After three years there, during which he became news editor, he moved to *The Times* as a reporter and, later, feature writer. In June 1973 he joined the first commercial radio station, the London Broadcasting Company.

Marcel Berlins and
Geoffrey Wansell

Caught in the Act

Children, Society and the Law

Penguin Books

Penguin Books Ltd, Harmondsworth,
Middlesex, England
Penguin Books Inc., 7110 Ambassador Road,
Baltimore, Maryland 21207, U.S.A.
Penguin Books Australia Ltd, Ringwood,
Victoria, Australia
Penguin Books Canada Ltd,
41 Steelcase Road West, Markham, Ontario, Canada
Penguin Books (N.Z.) Ltd,
182–190 Wairau Road, Auckland 10, New Zealand

First published 1974

Made and printed in Great Britain by
Hazell Watson & Viney Ltd,
Aylesbury, Bucks
Set in Monotype Times

Contents

Introduction

Juvenile delinquency is a subject which provokes everyone, affects many, but concerns few. About 200,000 children under seventeen in England and Wales are dealt with by the law after committing offences each year. Probably hundreds of thousands of others are never found out.

The problem of children in trouble is unquestionably of crucial importance to the whole of our society. It affects not just the delinquent child himself, but his family, school, friends and social environment, not to mention his victims, their families and social existence. Ignore a child's delinquency and he is potentially being abandoned to crime for the rest of his life. Yet for all its pervasive importance this issue has been remarkably little debated. In particular the law governing delinquent children is barely known, or, where known, often misunderstood.

This book grew out of a series of articles on children in trouble and the law in *The Times* late in 1972. We were conscious at that time that the complex issues we raised then needed longer and more detailed consideration, and were surprised – and somewhat disturbed – that this had, apparently, never been attempted except within the confines of debates between those professionally concerned with the problems. Too often this debate seemed to take the form of confrontation rather than objective and constructive discussion, whilst the general public remained largely unaware and unconcerned about it.

What struck us as important was the effect the law had on the hundreds of thousands of children and their parents who come into contact with it. We provide no hard and fast solutions to the problems we raise, but offer rather some suggestions which we hope might form a basis for discussion, not just among those who deal professionally with delinquent children – whether magistrates, judges, social workers, probation officers, local authorities, the staff of the residential homes to which these children are sent, civil servants or politicians – but among the general public, whom we believe ought to be better informed and more concerned.

We have not set out to write a detailed guide to the law and practice which governs the way society and its institutions treat children in trouble. There are already sufficient textbooks and professional handbooks doing just that. But we have attempted to provide an informed analysis of both the law and the practice, and to point out those areas in which these are deficient in dealing with the problems which they confront.

At present society tends to condemn, sometimes with real venom, its teenage vandals, its football hooligans or its young thieves. Yet it tragically neglects to offer any help to these children who most need it. As a result too many end up slipping into a life of adult crime. For delinquent children are often the children of the inadequate, the incompetent, the inarticulate, the poor and the many who neither understand society nor how to introduce their children to it. In common with the socially or physically deprived in other areas of need these parents and their children have consistently suffered from official neglect.

Of course there are laws and institutions to help them but most people simply remain unconcerned about delinquency among the young. They prefer to ignore it, hoping it will disappear – as their own delinquency as children may have done. But even where the laws are applied they are all too often inadequate.

What has emerged from this is an ambiguous and confusing legal framework for juvenile delinquency in this country, which underlines society's comparative lack of interest in it. Lip service is continually paid in the laws to helping delinquent children back to the path of righteousness, but these have been strikingly unsuccessful in combating the rising tide of juvenile crime. A new approach is urgently needed.

We have set out to suggest what might be done to help. In the long term the only certain cure for delinquency is to eradicate the social conditions from which it stems. This book cannot do that. But we believe that delinquent children need society's help more than the steady and the stable. More time, resources and public effort should be devoted to them, rather than to those whose parents offer the stability and love of a family. The delinquent child is the most needy member of his age group, not the least.

The most recent and significant legislative attempt to redress this balance was in 1969. The well-intentioned Children and Young Persons Act of that year tried to ensure that every child in trouble was treated as being in need of care rather than in need of punishment. This laudable ambition has not been realized in practice. Not only do some experts now believe that children can commit virtually any crime with impunity, but it is also clear that delinquent children, particularly the most difficult, disruptive and persistent ones, are today receiving no better help and care than they did before the Act came into force. This is still further evidence of the neglect they have always been shown by a society which is fundamentally embarrassed by their existence.

In order to avoid the awkwardness of the legal definitions we have throughout this book used the words 'children' and 'juveniles' to describe anyone under the age of seventeen. Where we have wanted to apply the legal definition of a child as someone aged under fourteen and a young person as someone of fourteen but under seventeen we have done so expressly. On occasion we have also used the words 'the Act' or 'the 1969 Act' as shorthand for the Children and Young Persons Act 1969. The term 'parent' is normally to be taken as including the possible alternative of 'guardian'. Although we have referred mainly to male child delinquents, most of what we argue applies equally to girls, and we are conscious of the increasing part they are playing in juvenile criminality.

Most of the former approved schools, remand homes, probation hostels and children's homes have already become part of the new community homes system, and the rest are expected to do so shortly. In future all these institutions are to be called community homes. But because of the varied nature of these institutions, and to try to escape from clumsy phrasing, we have tended to call them by their original names. Therefore where we refer to the approved schools, we mean community homes which were formerly approved schools.

In the course of preparing both the original articles in *The Times* and this book we have spoken to many people actively involved in and concerned with helping children in trouble. We would like to offer our thanks to all of them. It is perhaps invidious to single out any individuals, but we are especially grateful to Mr Joseph Brayshaw, the secretary of the Magistrates' Association, and Professor Winifred Cavenagh. We should also like to pay tribute to the many officials in the Department of Health and Social Security, the Home Office and New Scotland Yard for the guidance they have given to us.

This book would have been virtually impossible to write without the help of the library and archives of *The Times* and the encouragement and forbearance of our colleagues there.

Needless to say all the opinions expressed are our own and should not be associated with anyone else or with those of any group or organization.

The new Labour Government has not yet made clear whether it intends to take any action markedly different from the policy of its Conservative predecessor. Unfortunately, however, in the present economic climate it is unlikely that any government would place a high priority on the treatment of children in trouble.

Marcel Berlins and Geoffrey Wansell
London, April 1974

1 The Beginnings: Leg Irons to Leniency

Children have always got into trouble. It was not until the beginning of the industrial revolution, however, and the massive movement of population into the towns that children in trouble began to become a social problem, in which reformers and then governments began to concern themselves. Before that they had always been their parents' responsibility. The society as a whole took no interest.

But as during the eighteenth century the cities of England filled with the new urban poor, and the new factories and workshops provided large organizations not based on the family unit, so the conception of children being punished by society rather than their parents for their misdeeds grew.

By the beginning of the nineteenth century children caught stealing, by far the most common trouble they got into, were thought of as morally wicked and punished firmly for their evil-doing, by the society in the shape of the criminal courts. The notion that their crime could be the result of social deprivation was still a long way off, and the idea that the state might be responsible for ridding them of that deprivation even further away. If the children of the poor stole then they had to be punished for doing so, even if they stole because they were starving.

If the children of the rich stole, in the privacy of their own rural communities, a thrashing from their father was usually the only consequence.

So the children who got into trouble were almost always the children of the poor and they came from the cities of England, a pattern which has hardly changed in the ensuing two centuries.

Children in trouble in the new industrial England were dealt with swiftly. If they were lucky they were punished by the factory owner. If they were thought particularly bad then they were taken before the magistrate for a stiffer penalty. Indeed, they were treated in no way differently from adults.

Children were sent to prison where they slept and lived in exactly the same conditions as adults (for society did not accept that the moral responsibility of a child was less than that of a man). Children under twelve often became habitual offenders for the same reasons that the persistent adult offender often develops today – prison provided a home where he had none. In the midst of the poverty which was such a feature of the early industrial society prison provided one resting place for the many orphan, unwanted and abandoned unhappy children. (The handful of voluntary societies trying to help these children could no more than scrape the surface of the problem.)

The magistrates did not concern themselves with philosophizing on the causes of delinquency. For them a child that committed a crime was showing evidence of a grave moral failing, and the punishment needed to be severe. There were in the early part of the nineteenth century nearly 200 offences for which children could be sentenced to death. Although this penalty was in fact imposed relatively rarely, some of the alternatives were scarcely less grotesque – for example, transportation to the colonies.

It had been possible to transport children convicted of a crime to Australia since 1784, and earlier than that some had been sent to the West Indies. A child whose crime seemed to warrant the death penalty regularly had his sentence commuted to transportation. With so few choices of punishment available to the magistrate the pressure on places in the ships transporting children was intense. (It was equally intense among adults for very similar reasons.) Both children and adults awaiting transportation then were often condemned to spend months, and sometimes years, in one of the notorious 'hulks' of ships moored in the River Thames. The official argument in favour of these hideous institutions occurs again and again in the history of coping with children in trouble – criminals cannot be allowed to remain near the ordinary population in case their moral weakness (as shown by their crime) pollutes the morals of the law-abiding citizens.

The hulks became more and more numerous during the latter part of the eighteenth century. But at the same time the colonies' appetite for the transported, whether men or boys, began to decline. The objections from the colonies increased, and the hulks came to be prisons in their own right. At the beginning of the nineteenth century the hulks were the principal method of punishment for children found getting into trouble. Very young offenders might serve part of their sentences in one and then earn a 'ticket of leave', to enable them to get out. Many simply perished in them.

Only one of the hulks was reserved for children. Run by a notorious superintendent named Capper, it gained the reputation between 1823 and 1844 of being even worse than the adult hulks.

As transportation declined, and crime grew, it became increasingly important to find a way of deciding what could be done about children in trouble. For adults the answer was simple – build more prisons; and at the start of the nineteenth century the same answer still held good for children. Prisons at the time were still largely privately owned and administered, some by the local magistrates, and others by entrepreneurs who set up what were in effect prison businesses. The opportunities for forced labour by children were obvious.

At the beginning of the century all children went to the same prisons as the adults, but in 1838, under the influence of the flowering of liberalism in the newly wealthy middle class, came a significant development, the opening of a special prison solely for boys at Parkhurst.

The conditions at Parkhurst were poor, but the governors of the prison did at least attempt to experiment with the régime, and to classify the boys into different categories of offender. For the first time in penal history boys were grouped – there was, for example, a general ward for fourteen-year-olds and over, a junior ward for the under-fourteens, a probationary ward where all boys stayed for their first four months, a refractory ward for punishment and an infirmary ward for the sick.

The régime was a mixture of the old harsh methods and occasional attempts at reform. Conditions were progressive only in comparison with those of the adult prisons of the day. Leg irons were not removed for good conduct, for example, until 1843, and for the refractory there was whipping or a punishing bread and water diet.

In 1833, when transportation was finally declared illegal, there were 35,000 young people under twenty-one in prison, 10,000 of them under sixteen. But at the same time as there had been faltering experiments in the prison system so the efforts of the newly growing band of liberal reformers, many of them women, began to have its effect on the treatment of children in trouble.

A reformer of crucial importance in the history of children in trouble was Mary Carpenter. Religious, obstinate and canny, she showed all the great qualities of the nineteenth-century reformers, bullying and haranguing reform from sceptical and unwilling governments. She believed her mission was to save 'the children of the perishing and dangerous classes'. In 1851, in reformatory schools, she attacked the system of sending children to the adult prisons as doing little more than ensuring that they became persistent offenders, and urged that they be sent to reformatory schools instead.

In 1854 she got her way. The Reformatory Schools Act gave the courts power to send children to certain existing institutions, run by independent voluntary organizations (one was run by Mary Carpenter herself) rather than sending them to adult prison. The Act also allowed the Government to contribute to the running of the schools – a significant step to State intervention in helping children in trouble. The courts were allowed to commit a child to a reformatory school for not less than two years nor more than five years.

Three years later another attempt to help children was made, by the Industrial Schools Act 1857. The schools were designed to provide elementary education for the children of the poorer classes, and the courts were empowered to send children to them. Both the reformatories and the industrial schools remained under voluntary management, although they both received legal powers to detain children and were subject to government inspection. They were the first real attempts to care for children outside the prison system who had shown they needed help, either because they had committed crimes or because they were destitute.

The reformatories and industrial schools were by no means 'soft'. By today's standards they were rigid, disciplinarian and religion-orientated. But by the 1880s there were more than 200 of these schools in Britain, smaller than the prisons, and less overtly punitive. They were for the luckier minority of children in trouble. The rest, many thousands, still went to the adult prison, for a huge variety of offences, including throwing stones, breaking windows, playing pitch and toss, bathing in a canal, trespassing and, of course, stealing.

In 1895 the Gladstone Committee was appointed by the Government to look into the reformatories and industrial schools created forty years before. Its report reflected the change in public attitude that had gradually been taking place during that time. Children in trouble were seen, for the first time officially, as being the victims of society and their poverty, rather than as the perpetrators of evil actions. The need, in certain cases, to help rather than punish children was acknowledged.

By the turn of this century special courts were beginning to emerge, often under the influence of the Quaker families, designed to cope with cases involving children, and staffed by magistrates with particular interest in that field. In 1907, the Liberal Government, as part of its programme of social reform, passed the Probation of Offenders Act, which set out to reinforce the parents' control of their children with the help of social workers. Its stated objective was to avoid 'branding an offender whom the court may want to help rather than to damage with a mark which he will carry through life'.

The following year, 1908, however, saw the most fundamental change, The Children Act, often referred to as the Children's Charter. It accepted the principles set out in the Gladstone Committee's report and represented the official realization of the changing climate of opinion. In it the Liberal Asquith Government simply abolished imprisonment for children, ending a system that had lasted for 200 years.

The 1908 Act also established juvenile courts specially to deal with children in trouble, although it left unchanged – at seven – the age at which a child could legally be said to be criminally responsible for his actions. It was to be another quarter of a century, however, before these courts were primarily charged with the task of looking after the welfare of the children that appeared before them rather than considering the correct form of punishment. Nevertheless the 1908 Act represented a momentous change in the attitude to delinquent children.

The Act also charged the courts with a responsibility for the neglected rather than the naughty children who had committed crime. It empowered the new juvenile courts to send to an industrial court any child under fourteen found begging or destitute, without a parent or guardian, associating with thieves or prostitutes, or whose parents had drunken or criminal habits. It was the first official indication that the state was prepared to interfere in the privacy of family life to save children from being misused or harmed by their parents or their environment.

The Act also established the Children's Department of the Home Office to supervise the reformatories and the industrial schools as well as generally to keep a close watch on the treatment of children in trouble.

In the next twenty years it was the neglected rather than the naughty children who were to increasingly dominate official thinking about children in trouble. As the awareness grew that the distinction between the two types of children was difficult to maintain so the distinction between the two types of schools these children could be sent to – reformatories for the naughty and industrial schools for the younger and the obviously neglected – became increasingly pointless. In any case the use of these schools was declining, partly because of the increasing use of probation and partly because during the First World War young people in trouble were being sent to the trenches rather than to the schools.

In 1927 a Home Office Departmental Committee on the Treatment of Young Offenders finally formally accepted that the distinction between these two types of children was wrong. It marked the official death of the notion held so firmly in the eighteenth and nineteenth centuries that it was moral weakness which led to neglect, poverty and crime.

This remarkably radical report concluded that 'there is little or no difference in character and needs between the neglected and the delinquent child. It is often a mere accident whether he is brought before the court because he is wandering or beyond control, or because he has committed some offence. Neglect leads to delinquency.'

Just as the 1908 Act had been a watershed in the treatment of children convicted of committing crime, by abolishing imprisonment, so the Committee's report in 1927 was a watershed in the official attitude to children who needed help, whether or not they were delinquent. It pointed out that the courts were failing to provide the protection that was so often needed, and insisted that it was the court's job to look after children and not to punish them.

The Children and Young Persons Act 1933, based on the Committee's report, went a long way to abolishing the distinction between children who had done wrong and children who needed help. To start with, it abolished the distinction between the reformatories and the industrial schools – calling them both 'approved' by the Home Secretary. But more significantly it allowed an outside body to interfere in the family, if it thought a child was going wrong. By section 62, 'any local authority, constable or authorized person having reasonable ground for believing that a child or young person is in need of care or protection may bring him before a juvenile court'. It was a praiseworthy attitude, only let down in practice by the weakness of the institutions and organization available to give the child the 'care and protection' needed.

The Act's concept of care and protection as the principle to be applied by the juvenile courts still lies behind the system for coping with children in trouble today. Its effect was to bring before the courts children in need of care or protection from almost any cause, whether they were neglected, abandoned, exposed to moral danger, ill-disciplined or uncontrolled.

It also turned the courts into fundamentally an agency of giving help and not punishment. Section 44(1) stated

> Every court in dealing with a child or young person who is brought before it, either as being in need of care or protection or as an offender or otherwise, *shall have regard to the welfare of the child or young person* [our italics] and shall in a proper case take steps for removing him from undesirable surroundings, and for securing that proper provision is made for his education and training.

The distinction between the wicked or naughty child and the

neglected one, between the depraved and the deprived, was finally laid to rest, at least in theory.

In reality the institutions charged with looking after children who had come before the courts were still largely immersed in the old theories and attitudes. The voluntary bodies, whose work had been so significant in the nineteenth century, had not moved with the times, and they still controlled many of the schools.

The ways in which the local authorities carried out their new responsibilities under the 1933 Act varied remarkably from place to place. Some built cottage-style homes in pleasant rural settings, but many institutions often seemed unable to shake off the conception that they were little more than the reformatories, schools for bad children, with a change of name.

But it was possible to sympathize with the dilemma of the approved schools and indeed with many of the conflicts confronted by institutions helping both children convicted of crimes and those in need of help.

For, as the Ingleby Report on Children and Young Persons remarked forcefully nearly thirty years later, the 1933 Act meant that the juvenile courts had a confusing dual role. This not only confused the public, the parents and children brought before these courts, but also the institutions to which the children were sent.

As the Ingleby Committee pointed out

> The court remains a criminal court in the sense that it is a magistrates' court, that it is principally concerned with trying offences, that its procedure is a modified form of ordinary criminal procedure and that, with a few special provisions, it is governed by the law of evidence in criminal cases. Yet the requirement to have regard to the welfare of the child, and the various ways in which the court may deal with an offender suggest a jurisdiction, that is not criminal. It is not easy to see how the two principles can be reconciled ...

The debate about how to treat children in trouble has focused on that dilemma ever since the passing of the 1933 Act. It is still the crucial issue today.

The approved schools and the other institutions, including the new remand homes which local authorities had to provide for children waiting to be dealt with, had to accept both children who had been convicted of an offence and those who had merely been found in need of care and protection. The neglected and the naughty were inextricably involved with each other, and this tended to make those in need of care resentful and suspicious that they were being punished under the old theories rather than treated under the new. The attempts to resolve this confusion in the institutions as well as in the courts have continued unabated since then, and are still far from settled by the Children and Young Persons Act 1969.

The onset of war in 1939 tragically disrupted the already confused courts and institutions, armed with their new liberal principles but finding them difficult to put into practice. In 1940 the number of children being committed to the approved schools had gone up by almost 50 per cent on the last year of peace, and there was a rapid increase in the numbers of children coming before the juvenile courts. This new boom in offenders, however, simplified the dilemma – the schools and the courts mainly settled down in their old ways of treating everyone who came before them as basically naughty, as an offender. The institutions also retained their predilection for punishment. (It is worth recalling, for example, that it was only in 1938 that a committee on corporal punishment recommended the abolition of whipping for boys in the approved schools. It had decreased during the thirties, but some one per cent of boys were still being whipped in these schools – both offenders and those needing care and protection.)

The dismal conditions in the institutions coping with children in trouble, partly a result of lack of finance, but mainly stemming from their confusion about their role, continued throughout the war. By 1946 the Curtis Committee, another radical Home Office committee, had charted how bad things had become. The patchwork of elderly poor law institutions, little cottage homes, newly built barracks, submerged under the growing tide of delinquency brought on by the alienation and tumult of war made their report distinctly depressing. They recommended a number of major reforms.

Within two years two major pieces of legislation had emerged from the new Labour Government to help children in trouble.

But they only underlined the extraordinary confusion that had blighted this whole area for so long. On one hand the Children Act 1948 implemented the suggestions of the Curtis Committee, particularly by pledging the local authorities' new Children's Departments to take into their care children considered by the courts as needing it. But at the same time the Criminal Justice Act 1948 increased the penal element in the system for dealing with some children. For although it abolished imprisonment entirely for the under-seventeens, it introduced detention centres and attendance centres, both institutions bearing many of the marks of the prison system. The Government also introduced the now notorious remand centres for young people over seventeen (and for 'unruly' younger ones), although it was more than a decade before the first of these was to be opened at Ashford in Middlesex. The clear implication of the Criminal Justice Act was that many children in trouble really needed a dose of discipline rather than the system of care and protection that had begun to emerge before the war.

The sternness of the reaction of the Labour Government to the juvenile delinquency of the post-war period has provided a touchstone for much of the debate about helping children in trouble since then. Continually attempts to suggest that a child convicted of an offence is the victim of his society have been countered by arguments stressing the need for discipline.

During the 1950s the ambiguous approach of the legislation designed to deal with children became more and more obvious.

In October 1956, Major Gwilym Lloyd George, then Home Secretary, acknowledged the confusion by appointing another government committee. Like its distinguished predecessors in 1895 and 1927 it produced a cogent and progressive report, but unlike the others, it was virtually ignored by the Government. The Ingleby Committee on Children and Young Persons reported in 1960 after visiting institutions and examining 151 witnesses. Significantly it recommended forcefully that the age of criminal responsibility should be raised from the eight which the 1933 Act had laid down, to twelve and then to thirteen or fourteen.

Echoing the proposals of the 1927 Committee, the Ingleby Committee recommended that for children the juvenile courts should move away from their traditional criminal role as courts and become increasingly agencies to decide what help could best be given to a child coming before it. In effect it suggested that children who committed a crime were just as much in need of care as those formally put into local authority care by the courts. Its suggestion to eliminate all the younger children from the criminal law by raising the age limit would have had the effect of doing exactly this.

For the younger children the Ingleby Committee recommended: 'There should be a new procedure for children under twelve who commit offences and for all children who are in need of care or protection or are beyond control as at present defined. All such children should be brought to court as being "in need of protection or discipline".'

The Conservative Government, in the Children and Young Persons Act 1963, watered down the Committee's proposals until they were so diluted as to be of very limited effect. They at first declined to raise the age of criminal responsibility at all, and only raised it to ten during the debate on the 1963 Bill, after a profound disagreement in the House of Lords which ended in its defeat. The 1963 Act also empowered, for the first time, local authorities to spend money to prevent delinquency. But because of a shortage of funds and staff very little was done.

The 1963 Act left the courts and the institutions, largely unreformed for thirty years, still saddled with the confusion over their role. The trace of the Victorian notion that children who were convicted of offences were morally reprehensible and therefore should be punished still hung in the air.

The Act only marginally amended the old definition of its predecessor thirty years earlier, by expanding the definition of those children who needed care from 'care and protection' to 'care, protection and control'. This change missed the point of the Ingleby Committee's recommendation, which was designed to do away with the criminal element in the helping of children in trouble. The Act left the courts still trapped in the difficult task of having at one and the same time to help and to punish children coming before it, often the very same children. And to do so in the same institutions, mainly the approved schools.

2 'A Challenge to Us All?' The Longford Report and After

In the early sixties, following the Ingleby Report and despite the disappointing 1963 Act, the trend was towards more care and protection. In 1964 the Labour Party published a research pamphlet, *Crime – a Challenge to Us All*, the most important statement yet from those holding the view that children in trouble, whether delinquent or not, should be cared for and treated, and not punished. The report was the product of several months' intensive effort by a distinguished study group led by Lord Longford. Members of the group included Beatrice Serota, who as Baroness Serota later became Minister for Health, Lord Gardiner, who shortly afterwards became Lord Chancellor, and Professor Terence Morris, the noted criminologist.

From the point of view of the Government's approach to the treatment of children in trouble the most significant member of the Longford study group was Miss Alice Bacon who, only weeks after the publication of the report, was named as Minister of State at the Home Office with direct responsibility for the Children's Department when the Labour Party took office.

The Longford group's attitude was far removed from the traditional approach to delinquency:

> Chronic or serious delinquency in a child is, in the main, we believe, evidence of lack of the care, the guidance and the opportunities to which every child is entitled. There are very few children who do not behave badly at times; but the children of parents with ample means rarely appear before juvenile courts. The machinery of law is reserved mainly for working-class children who, more often than not, are also handicapped by being taught in too big classes in unsatisfactory school buildings with few amenities or opportunities for out of school activities.
>
> Anti-social behaviour in a child may arise from difficulties at home, from unhappiness at school, from physical or mental handicaps or maladjustment, or from a variety of other causes for which the child has no personal responsibility.

The Longford Report advocated the establishment of a family service to look after all children who might need care. It argued that this service should help to prevent children coming before the courts or being taken into care by local authorities. It was the logical extension of the arguments that lay behind the 1933 and 1963 Children and Young Persons Acts, but taken to their extreme.

The Longford study group noted:

> It is a truism that a happy and secure family life is the foundation of a healthy society and the best safeguard against delinquency and anti-social behaviour. Many pay lip-service to this belief; all too little has been done seriously to attempt its realization.

It suggested that the new family service might incorporate responsibilities of some of the children's, health and welfare departments. It was seen as supporting and supplementing the efforts of parents and the schools. The group also suggested a new central department should be established within the Home Office consisting of social workers and administrators as well as civil servants. This was another sign of the group's conviction that the courts, magistrates and penal-style institutions were inappropriate to the treatment of children in trouble.

The report's conclusions also contained a recommendation for

> many more reception and observation homes for children who would hitherto have been sent to remand homes, and more remand homes for the older age-group. Here the most difficult children and young people, many of them mentally and emotionally disturbed, will be able to stay for a sufficient length of time for their home problems and behaviour difficulties to be studied by skilled staff.

The study group felt that family courts, to replace the existing juvenile and magistrates' courts dealing with children, would forestall much delinquency. These would become properly constituted courts of law, bound by the same rules of evidence as the existing courts. 'The emphasis and atmosphere of the court will, however, be essentially human: the welfare of the family as a whole will be a primary consideration.'

The group also made another fundamental suggestion for reform which had been skirted around persistently in the preceding fifty years. They argued that the age of criminal responsibility should be raised dramatically – to coincide with the statutory school-leaving age. It had become ten in the Children and Young Persons Act 1963 in England and Wales, but was still eight in Scotland.

The report suggested that the schools should largely be amalgamated in a national plan for all residential establishments designed to treat children in need of care, whether they were in trouble or not, thus foreshadowing the changes in the approved school system which the 1969 Act would bring about. The Longford group did not neglect to emphasize the importance of recruiting sufficient social workers and ancillaries to support their suggestions, but did so at the end of their report, a long way from the main conclusions. The group felt it was not impossible to recruit sufficient people, given 'the will, the drive and the financial resources'.

When the Labour Government came into power on its narrow majority a matter of weeks later the report was still reverberating in the minds of everyone concerned in dealing with delinquent children. It had created an atmosphere of change, and one which was based on the growing feeling among many sections of the population that punishment was no longer the correct approach for a civilized society to take towards its children in trouble.

Within a year the Government had translated the ideas of the Longford group into a White Paper, whose suggestions were to become the subject of a bitter controversy. *The Child, the Family and the Young Offender*, as the White Paper was called, was published in August 1965. As Lord Kilbrandon's Committee on Children and Young Persons in Scotland had already been broadly accepted by the Government, the plans laid out in the White Paper were only for England and Wales.

Its laudable statement of intent was the same that has appeared in almost every proposal to help children in trouble – if crime by the young can be contained, the problem of crime among adults will be lessened. 'The prospect of success, and its rewards, are greatest with young offenders,' it stated.

The White Paper went on to paraphrase many of the Longford proposals. In particular it accepted the Longford argument that there should be a family service within the local authorities trying to prevent children coming before the courts.

On the raising of the age of criminal responsibility, the Longford group commented, voicing the opinion of many reformers:

> No understanding parent can contemplate without repugnance the branding of a child in early adolescence as a criminal, whatever offence he may have committed. If it is a trivial one, such a procedure is indefensible; if a more serious charge is involved this is, in itself, evidence of the child's need for skilled help and guidance . . . We believe that in justice to our children, and for the health and well-being of society, no child in early adolescence should have to face criminal proceedings: these children should receive the kind of treatment they need, without any stigma or any association with the penal system.

This philosophy was to form the basis of the Labour Government's attitude to the treatment of children in trouble for the remainder of their period in office.

The White Paper was charged with considering the treatment of young people up to the age of twenty-one, and suggested that the usual distinction drawn between those under seventeen and those between seventeen and twenty-one should be changed. In its place it argued that sixteen should be the dividing line. For the under-sixteen, the White Paper felt the whole panoply of the law and the courts was irrelevant.

In its most direct reform it suggested: 'Children should be spared the stigma of criminality.' It went on to argue that

> In the great majority of cases of offenders brought before the juvenile courts, the facts are not in dispute. The problem is to decide the appropriate treatment, and the court procedures, designed essentially for testing evidence, do not provide the best means for directing social inquiries and discussing possibilities with the child's parents and the social services that might be concerned with treatment.

It went on,

> A child under sixteen who has done an act which is an offence in the case of an older person or who is in need of care, protection or control will be brought before a local family council, a number of which will be appointed for each local authority area. The council will endeavour to reach agreement with the parents of the child on the treatment to be

supplied. If the facts are in dispute or agreement cannot be reached on treatment, the issue will be referred to a court for determination.

Then it continued,

Special magistrates' courts will be set up which, sitting as family courts will, in respect of children under sixteen, determine disputed issues of fact or decide treatment when agreement cannot be reached between the family council and the child's parents . . .

The White Paper made it perfectly clear that the magistrates' role was to end there, by stating:

If the treatment required for a child under sixteen involves removal from home, the child will be placed in the care of the local authority, and sent to an appropriate children's home or other institution, or placed in a foster-home. This treatment could be varied as required, with the object of returning him to his home as soon as progress justified it. Approved school will cease to form a system separate from other children's homes.

The first purpose of the proposed changes, it said, was

to take children and young persons under the age of sixteen as far as possible outside the ambit of criminal law and of the courts, and to make, if possible with the agreement of their parents or guardians, such arrangements for their welfare as are appropriate.

But the Government did not commit itself firmly to the White Paper's proposals, even stating that they were only 'provisional' and adding that they were being published for the 'purposes of discussion before legislation is prepared'. In the circumstances this caution proved well founded. The suggestion that the juvenile courts should be abandoned provoked a flood of controversy, particularly arousing the magistracy, who argued that their experience in the treatment of children was being treated as of no account.

Many admitted, however, that the courts' dual role of treatment and the rule of law sometimes created difficulties. The dilemma is summed up neatly by Professor W. Cavenagh, in *Juvenile Courts, the Child and the Law*, when she states,

The most important question, therefore, is perhaps not whether to deal with young offenders in criminal or civil courts or through welfare boards as such, but how, under whatever system is in use, to ensure that the public is protected from crime, that liberty is preserved, and that the young offender gets the treatment he needs.

The Ingleby Committee had already grappled with the dilemma of the juvenile court's attempts to concern itself with treatment in the context of a criminal court. It had advocated a compromise, with the juvenile court retained, but more younger offenders being the subject of civil proceedings, by raising the age of criminal responsibility first to twelve and later to thirteen or fourteen.

The Ingleby Committee had foreseen a system in which the juvenile courts would eventually be entirely superseded, but the 1963 Children and Young Persons Act – brought in as a result of the report – fell far short of its proposals, although it did lay the groundwork for a reduction in the work of the courts by stating in section 1 that the local authority had a duty to do preventive work to reduce the need to bring children before the court at all.

A similar antipathy to the juvenile courts was also obvious from the report, in 1964, of the Committee on the Treatment of Children and Young Persons in Scotland, under the chairmanship of Lord Kilbrandon, which had advocated that the courts should be abolished, and replaced by juvenile panels of lay people appointed by the sheriff in the area after nomination by the education authority. Behind this panel was to be a new social education department, responsible for the preparation of social background reports, treatment recommendations and the subsequent application of treatment. Cases referred to the panel were to be dealt with by a 'reporter', qualified in law and experienced in administration, who would present the case and act as legal adviser. If there was a dispute about the panel's decisions, the disputed matter would go before the sheriff's court. The panel would have available to it a variety of measures, including cautioning the parent, admonishing the child, supervision, reception into the care of a local authority, and attendance at an attendance centre. The Social Work (Scotland) Act 1968 implemented these proposals almost in their entirety.

But there was not seen to be any necessary contradiction between the two approaches, juvenile panels in Scotland, and courts in England and Wales, as most authorities accepted that the juvenile courts in Scotland had not developed in the same way as those south of the border and did not and could not fulfil the same functions.

A formidable array of criticism descended on the proposals of *The Child, the Family and the Young Offender*. Professor Cavenagh, for example, produced two fundamental arguments, the first about the shortage of resources that beset any attempts to treat children who got into trouble: 'The formidable lack of resources will not be affected by the setting up of family councils, though it may well appear to become even more acute as more needs are revealed.' The other, based on the need for the experience of the magistracy, particularly in the criminal cases, centred on the proposal that treatment should be agreed with the parents. This, she said, did not seem to have in mind the

> type of parent commonly seen in the juvenile court, muddled, inadequate, beaten, pathetic, or truculent. Agreement, disagreement, and discussion are not very realistic terms to describe the part to be played by such families which appear before the family councils.

In the end arguments on these lines were to prevail. In April 1968 the Government, by then firmly established in the middle of its period of office, produced a new White Paper, *Children in Trouble*. It rejected the earlier suggestions to abolish the juvenile courts, although it accepted some of the Longford, Ingleby and Kilbrandon attitudes to the problems raised by juvenile delinquency. The new White Paper stated:

> It is probably a minority of children who grow up without ever misbehaving in ways which may be contrary to the law. Frequently such behaviour is no more than an incident in the pattern of a child's normal development. But sometimes it is a response to unsatisfactory family or social circumstances, a result of boredom in and out of school, an indication of maladjustment or immaturity, or a symptom of a deviant, damaged or abnormal personality.

It went on in the next paragraph to add, 'It has become increasingly clear that social control of harmful behaviour by the young, and social measures to help and protect the young, are not distinct and separate processes.'

It attempted the almost impossible, a compromise between the suggestions of the other reports and the retention of the legal powers of the juvenile courts. It rejected, therefore, the proposals for family courts, and also the suggestion that sixteen should be the dividing line between the two ages for treatment in the courts.

Children in Trouble in its turn, however, advocated a new form of procedure for offenders aged between ten and fourteen. This new process, it stated,

> will narrow down the circumstances in which court proceedings are now possible. It represents a half-way stage between care, protection or control proceedings and prosecution. It is designed to encourage parents to fulfil the responsibilities which are properly theirs, and to ensure that the child's home background is considered before a decision is taken whether court proceedings should be instituted. Proceedings will remain possible where they are necessary for the protection of society or for the sake of the child.

It was a compromise between the views of the earlier White Paper and the bitter criticisms some of its provisions had attracted. In its turn this proposal was to attract just as much criticism.

It suggested that committing an offence would cease to be a reason, by itself, for bringing a child to court. Where proceedings were necessary, it argued, they should be for care, protection or control; and the White Paper proposed that committing an offence should be added to the list of circumstances specified in the Children and Young Persons Act 1963 which would justify an order being made for the child to be placed in care.

For children between fourteen and seventeen the White Paper suggested that if an offence was admitted the course of action to be taken would be more complicated. The police would have to consult the children's department. Available information about the child's background would be considered and more information gathered if necessary. In some cases court proceedings would be decided upon, in others informal action, or in others care proceedings. But no prosecution would be brought under this procedure until a magistrate had decided that one of the statutory criteria had been met.

Children in Trouble went on to state that it was necessary to develop the facilities for observation and assessment of children and to increase the range of places for treatment, whether residential or not. In consequence it stated that the approved school order would be abolished in the juvenile court (this was also proposed, of course, in *The Child, the Family and the Young Offender*). It suggested there should be a new form of intermediate treatment between supervision in the home and committal to care (an entirely new proposal at that time) and argued that all supervision of children under fourteen should be done by the local authority, and not the probation service.

As a result of these changes the White Paper suggested that the name approved schools should be dropped entirely, and all local authority children's homes and hostels, remand homes, reception and remand centres, local authority and voluntary approved schools and some voluntary children's homes should be called collectively 'the public system of community homes for children in the care of local authorities'. Joint Planning Committees would prepare plans for the comprehensive development of all the homes in their area.

3 Delinquents into Criminals

The Children and Young Persons Bill, which followed closely the White Paper proposals, was first debated in Parliament in March 1969. Introducing it, the Home Secretary, Mr James Callaghan, stated its aim – 'to prevent the deprived and delinquent children of today from becoming the deprived, inadequate, unstable or criminal citizens of tomorrow'.

This would be done, he said,

> first, as a matter of social philosophy, as well as a practical matter, to build on the family and on the parents, to try to ensure that they assume the major responsibility for the welfare, control, care and discipline of their children . . . Secondly, where the family and the parents cannot succeed without help, to provide effective support for those families through the social and other services which in such cases must supplement the efforts of the parents.
>
> Thirdly, by these means to keep out of the courts all those children who will benefit as much, or more, from other treatment as they will by going to court . . . fourthly, to ensure as nearly as we can real equality for all children of all classes and backgrounds.

The Bill was not designed solely with children who committed offences in mind. It dealt also with non-offenders who suffered from various disadvantages. But it was the way in which child offenders were dealt with that provoked almost all the controversy and where all the important changes in the law and procedure were to be found.

It became clear from the outset that whilst the Conservative opposition, led by Mr Quintin Hogg, were in some sympathy with the Bill's objectives, and agreed with many of its provisions, there was fundamental disagreement about those parts of the Bill which related to the role to be played by the juvenile court in dealing with child offenders. As a result of these differences, the Conservatives opposed some clauses of the Bill all the way through its Parliamentary passage.

The disagreements were over crucial issues. One of the principal objects of the Bill was to provide a procedure for raising the minimum age at which a child could be liable to criminal proceedings from ten to fourteen, as recommended in *Children in Trouble.*

The Labour Government intended to raise the age at which a child would be liable to having criminal proceedings taken against him gradually. At first, in what is now section 4, which states that 'a person shall not be charged with an offence, except homicide, by reason of anything done or committed while he was a child', the Secretary of State would, by order, define a child as one who had reached eleven. He could make orders raising this age until it eventually, after several years, reaches fourteen. But even this gradual approach was not palatable to the Conservatives.

It should be noted that none of this would change the age of criminal responsibility as such. That would remain at ten. It was the steps which could be taken against a child which would be affected. The procedure which was to take the place of a criminal prosecution against children under fourteen, and could also be used as an alternative to criminal proceedings for those between fourteen and seventeen is set out in what is now section 1 of the Act. It instituted a new system of care proceedings for both offenders and non-offending children in need.

Clause 1 of the Bill, now section 1 of the Act, gave a juvenile magistrate the power to make a number of orders in respect of the child if he was of the opinion that any of the following conditions are satisfied.

(a) his proper development is being avoidably prevented or neglected or his health is being avoidably impaired or neglected or he is being ill-treated; or
(b) it is probable that the condition set out in the preceding paragraph will be satisfied in his case, having regard to the fact that the court or another court has found that that condition is or was satisfied in the case of another child or young person who is or was a member of the household to which he belongs; or
(c) he is exposed to moral danger; or
(d) he is beyond the control of his parents or guardian; or
(e) he is of compulsory school age within the meaning of the Education

Act 1944, and is not receiving efficient full-time education suitable to his age, ability and aptitude; or

(f) he is guilty of an offence, excluding homicide, and also that he is in need of care or control which he is unlikely to receive unless the court makes an order . . .

Where any of these conditions are satisfied the magistrate is empowered to make a care order, thereby placing the child in the care of the local authority; a supervision order, a hospital order, or a guardianship order, or the magistrate could require the child's parents to enter into a recognisance to take proper care of him and exercise proper control over him.

Many of the conditions are not new, and are similar to those which justified a 'fit person order' under the Children and Young Persons Act 1963.

But the 'offence' condition (f), was new and was specifically put in so that the juvenile court could deal with more children under the 'care' procedure rather than through criminal proceedings. It was a clear expression of the Act's desire to keep children under fourteen away from criminal proceedings of any kind.

Taking the case of a child who commits an offence, Section 1 means that not only does the offence have to be proved against him beyond a reasonable doubt (a later provision specifically lays down that the usual criminal standard of proof is to be used) but it must then also be shown that he is in need of care or control which he is unlikely to get from his parents or family.

Much of the debate in Parliament was taken up with comparing the cases of two children under fourteen committing identical offences. One coming from a 'good' middle-class home with articulate, adequate and relatively affluent parents, would probably not be brought before the court at all, because the second half of the proof requirement, that he would not receive the necessary care unless an order were made, would probably not be satisfied. The child from a deprived area and inadequate family, on the other hand, would be brought before the court and a care order was likely to be made against him. This, the Conservatives in Parliament and the Magistrates Association outside it, felt would be unfair.

Their basic objection was that many children under fourteen who committed offences were not in fact deprived or in need of the treatment proposed. These children, however, would, under the new legislation, escape the law altogether, because the offence alone was no longer enough to allow the court to take action.

The attempt to keep children as much as possible out of the courts and to switch the emphasis from criminal to care proceedings was also clear from the Bill's provisions for the fourteen- to seventeen-year-olds. Clause 5 set out an elaborate machinery to be followed before criminal proceedings could be instituted. It specified the category of persons who would be entitled to lay any information against a child in that age group and listed a number of steps which had to be taken before any prosecution could get under way. Under this section the police are given a responsibility for deciding whether to start criminal proceedings (but it also required them to consult the local authority before making that decision). As it was originally drafted, the Bill, following *Children in Trouble*, left the final decision up to a juvenile court magistrate. This was amended during the progress of the Bill through Parliament, but even the watered-down form, cutting out the magistrates' role in the initial decision to take criminal proceedings, represents a clear invitation to use the courts as little as possible except for 'care' proceedings.

Clause 7 of the Bill raised the minimum age rendering a person eligible for Borstal from fifteen to seventeen (although this too was to take effect in stages, one year at a time) and also provided that the Secretary of State could take away from the juvenile courts their power to send a child to an attendance or detention centre. The running down of these centres and the abolition of Borstal for under-seventeens was again part of the philosophy behind the Bill of making as many child offenders as possible the subject of care and treatment rather than discipline and punishment.

The 1969 Bill also provided for magistrates to be given the power to make a new kind of supervision order, both for care or criminal proceedings, which would take the place of the old supervision orders and probation orders. The supervision would be carried out by a local authority social worker (or in some, relatively few, cases by a probation officer). An important new element in the role of the supervisor was to be the provision of facilities for 'intermediate treatment'. Based on the theory that a child could well benefit by 'constructive activities' which his environment normally would not give him, the supervisor was given power to send the child to participate in such activities as were available and suitable. The 'intermediate treatment' envisaged ranged from an evening a week with the local scouts to two or three months on an adventure farm.

Part 2 of the Bill contained provisions for the accommodation of children placed in the care of the local authority. It established regional planning committees (of which there are eleven in England and one in Wales) which have the duty of preparing plans for providing 'community homes' which can be used where necessary to place children placed in the authority's care, whether as a result of care or criminal proceedings. (Special provisions were made for voluntary organizations running children's homes or approved schools to join the community homes system, whilst still retaining responsibility for their own homes.) All the plans drawn up by the regional committees had to be approved by the Secretary of State. As a result of the provision of the community homes system, the names 'approved schools', 'remand homes', 'probation hostels' and 'probation homes' would cease to exist officially, and all would be known as community homes. What progress has been made with the community homes system and the regional plans is discussed in a later chapter.

Had the Children and Young Persons Act, which received the Royal Assent on 22 October 1963 been implemented as a whole there is little doubt that it would have succeeded at least in some way in treating very many juvenile delinquents (in common with children in trouble for other reasons) as in need of care and treatment rather than some form of punishment or disciplining. It would have gone some way towards achieving the aims of *Children in Trouble*.

The general election of 1970, however, unexpectedly put the Conservative Party in power and the Government found itself committed to the implementation of an Act major parts of which it had bitterly opposed when in opposition. The Government did a very simple thing to get itself out of this dilemma. It announced that it would not be implementing those parts of the Act with which it disagreed. A number of key sections are therefore not in force today. The Government has said it will not implement some of them at all. On others it has 'reserved its position'.

The unimplemented sections were, in many respects, the crucial ones to the philosophy of the Act. Section 4 is not to come into force, thus keeping the minimum age for criminal prosecution at ten. Section 5, which laid out the procedure to be followed before criminal proceedings could be started, has also not been brought into force.

Because sections 4 and 5 are not in operation, therefore, care proceedings for a child who had committed an offence became virtually a dead letter. As a delinquent child from ten onwards can still be brought to the court on criminal proceedings, why should anyone bother to use the complex care procedure which requires not only proof of the offence, but also proof that the child cannot receive adequate care at home? The same argument applies to the fourteen- to seventeen-year-olds. As the procedure had not been changed to make criminal proceedings more difficult, why not do exactly as before?

This has meant that apart from no longer being able to make an order directly sending a child to an approved school, the magistrates now have much the same powers as they had before the Act – which was certainly not the intention of the legislation. Equally, because the minimum age for Borstal was not raised to seventeen or even to sixteen, magistrates can still commit fifteen- and sixteen-year-olds to the Crown Courts for sentencing to those institutions. They can also continue to send children to detention centres and attendance centres for the foreseeable future.

The new care orders are not all that different from the old fit person orders nor are the new supervision orders that different from the old supervision and probation orders, apart from the introduction of intermediate treatment.

Those parts of the Act dealing with the new community homes system, regional plans and intermediate treatment have been largely implemented. But these were envisaged as being complementary to and dependent on the proposed shift away from criminal proceedings and towards care and protection, which has only partially taken place.

4 The Police: a Clash of Roles?

If a child gets into trouble now, therefore, he will come into contact with the law. He will be cautioned or prosecuted by police officers, whether in juvenile bureaux or not, and will probably appear before the juvenile court's magistrates. He may see a local authority social worker before he goes to court, or the magistrates may decide that he should be placed in their care when he appears.

If he is aged fourteen then he may be placed under the supervision of a probation officer or a social worker. They will then decide what help and treatment best suit him. But the court may decide in the older child's case that he should spend some of his Saturdays at an attendance centre (although younger children can be sent to them as well). Until the age of fifteen he may also be sent to the stricter régime of a junior detention centre for three months or, if he has turned fifteen, be committed to the Crown Court for sentence to a borstal.

But the court may decide for any child that none of these treatments are correct, preferring instead simply to discharge him absolutely or conditionally, bind over his parents to make sure that he behaves himself in future, or fine him or his parents. In fact more than half the children who finally appear before the courts are dealt with like this, and it should be recalled that only about six children out of every ten discovered doing something wrong by the police even get to court.

We propose to explain this system by dealing with the agencies and individuals that a child getting into trouble may encounter, starting with his being caught by the police and ending up with the residential institutions in which he may eventually find himself.

The police's attitude to juvenile crime, and their ways of dealing with it, differs from area to area. Most of the forty-seven police authorities, however, have now established separate

Juvenile Bureaux whose specific job is to deal with children. As an example we have taken the procedure used when a child is caught apparently committing an offence in the area of the Metropolitan Police in London. This procedure may differ in detail from other forces but the principles and approach that it embodies lie behind them all.

When a police officer discovers a juvenile under seventeen who is apparently committing an offence, or who appears to have just done so, the child will immediately be taken to a police station where the first important decision about his future is taken – whether or not to charge him at that stage. The police have a discretion in this, but will in general be guided by the principle that children should not be charged there and then unless this is unavoidable. A formal charge sets into motion a machinery which it is hard to stop and for that reason it is obviously desirable to have as much information as possible about both the child and the alleged offence before taking that step. But often, at that stage, information about the child himself, his family and his environment is sketchy or even non-existent. Further, the circumstances surrounding the offence are rarely known except in broad outline.

However, reluctant as the police genuinely are to charge a juvenile at the police station, in some circumstances they have no alternative. First, the offender will be charged if the offence is a serious one, that is, where it appears inevitable that a charge will eventually have to be made irrespective of what is subsequently found out about the child. Extreme cases of violence are an obvious example. Secondly, a charge will have to be made, by law, where the juvenile is arrested with an adult who is himself charged. Thirdly, the police will, again reluctantly, charge a juvenile where they have been unable to find the child's parents or guardian to take responsibility (or where the parents or guardian refuse to do so). In these cases the police charge the child because it is the only way in which they can make arrangements with the relevant social services departments for the child to be looked after whilst the parents are traced, or in some cases, more permanently. In cases which do not involve these three types of cases the practice of the police is usually that the child not be charged there and then. In most cases the parents are sent for and the child is allowed to go home with them.

In the meantime the station officer has been assessing whether the evidence that the child has in fact committed the alleged offence is credible. In many cases there may be little doubt – the child has been caught red-handed – but there are many other cases where the evidence is by no means clear. If the station officer is not satisfied as to the evidence against the child the chances are that the case will go no further. The boy and his parents will hear nothing more of the incident and the file will be closed. If on the other hand the offence clearly appears to have been committed by the boy, and he has not been charged, the papers are sent to the police Juvenile Bureau for the area, which will make the final decision about what to do with him.

These Juvenile Bureaux are recent additions to the police structure. The Metropolitan Police's bureaux were introduced over the whole London area in 1969. Now twenty-three police divisions have their own separate Juvenile Bureau and the other two divisions share another's facilities. The Chief Inspector in charge of a bureau is directly responsible to the Commander of the division and to the Commander of the Metropolitan district's Community Relations department at New Scotland Yard. This has the unenviable dual responsibility for the relationship between the police and the public, including race relations, and children in trouble. The London juvenile bureaux are staffed by a total of about 170 men and women police officers.

The role of this new branch of the police is crucial to the whole question of how we deal with our child offenders, for it is at this stage that decisions are made which may have profound consequences over the child's future.

The ultimate task of the bureau is to make decisions as to how juveniles accused of committing offences are to be dealt with. On receipt of the report from the police station to which the juvenile was originally brought, the bureau tries to find out as much as possible about him or her and to do this it asks the local authority social services department, the probation service and the local education authority for any information they may have about the child. (Liaison between the police and these authorities is happily on the increase in spite of the non-implementation of section 5 of the 1969 Act, which would have made it obligatory by law.) The bureau will at the same time also obtain fuller information about the offence alleged to have been committed.

If the Juvenile Bureau officer does not feel that the case has been proved it will be taken no further. If on the other hand he is convinced that the child in question has in fact committed the offence he will initiate a 'home inquiry'.

There have therefore already been two stages at which a decision had been taken not to proceed because the evidence is not thought to be strong enough – at the police station and at the juvenile bureau. The police will in theory not proceed with a prosecution against a juvenile unless they are sure of the child's guilt, beyond all reasonable doubt.

It is the home inquiry which best shows up the dual, and some would say conflicting, function of the police in dealing with juvenile offenders. In effect the police constable (or woman police constable) carrying out the inquiry is trying to set aside the law enforcement part of his duties and to take on the role of a social agency. His or her job is now, by visiting the home (in plain clothes) and speaking to the parents and the child, to find out why the child committed the offence, and to report on the home and family relationships and environment. The home inquiry report will then be submitted to the Chief Inspector in charge of the bureau who will also have studied the reports he has received from the social services, probation and education authorities. The next decision is now his.

Broadly, three alternatives are open to him – to officially caution the child, to charge him, or to do neither and take no further action. Taking the last mentioned first, there are a variety of reasons why the chief inspector may decide to drop the case. Often the social reports may suggest that the child is best left to the social services department. Or it might be that no action is taken against one of a group of co-offenders (all equally guilty) because the police do not wish to proceed against the others and do not wish to give the appearance of discrimination. In 1972, in London, of the approximately 30,000 children who had committed offences, about 3,000, some 10 per cent, had no further action taken against them. (In some cases, of course, this could be interpreted as meaning that the child had in effect been wrongly arrested, but these cases do not form a significant proportion. The vast majority are cases where the arrest was justified but the circumstances suggested that taking no action was the best way of handling it.)

The main alternatives usually faced by the Chief Inspector of the Juvenile Bureau are whether to charge a child or to administer an official caution. The police have a complete discretion in making this decision. Obviously some factors play a large part in helping them reach their decision. For instance, and this is a matter of common sense, a juvenile who has never before come to the notice of the police is more likely to be cautioned than to be taken to court. Another important factor (encountered at various stages in the process of dealing with delinquents) is the desire to appear to be treating co-offenders equally. So if a first offender gets into trouble with another boy who has been in some trouble before, it might seem logical to treat the latter with more severity than the former. But in fact this type of case has been shown to cause great bitterness on the part of the child more harshly treated ('Both of us did it together') and his parents, and can on occasion lead to an attitude of resentment towards the law and the law enforcement agencies which never disappears. So the police often have to be over-lenient with one of the children and caution him where logically he should have been proceeded against.

Before the Chief Inspector decides on an official caution the child must have clearly admitted the offence. If he disputes it there is no alternative but to charge him and let the court decide. Secondly, the parents must also have accepted the child's admission of guilt. Finally, the victim of the offence (if any) must agree to allow the police to deal with the offender in this way. (Unless the child is found guilty by a court, neither he nor his parents can be ordered to pay compensation for loss incurred by the victim. By agreeing to the caution the loser effectively gives up his right to recover compensation, other than by lengthy and costly civil action.)

If a caution is decided upon, it is administered by a uniformed

Superintendent or Chief Inspector (other than the one who took the decision to caution). It is mainly intended to be used against a first offender, to deter him from any future crime. It is a formal, slightly frightening, awe-inspiring occasion designed to bring home to the child and his parents the seriousness of the act the child has committed. But, depending on the circumstances of the case and what is known about the child and his family, the caution can range from a sympathetic and understanding chat and an attempt at reasoning and explanation to an army-style authoritarian ticking-off. The cautioning officer may in fact concentrate his attention more on the parents than the child, if he feels the fault lies mainly with them, and may sometimes see and talk to them separately.

In 1972, more than 10,000 children – more than one-third of the total number of young offenders detected in London, were dealt with in this way. It is difficult to assess what success the caution has in preventing the child offending again. It is clear from the available statistics that most children cautioned do not offend again, at any rate soon afterwards. But it should not be forgotten that a very large proportion of those cautioned would probably not have offended again anyway, caution or not.

There remains the category of offenders about whom the juvenile bureau head decided that court proceedings is the only possibility, and action is then taken by way of summons to bring them before the court. Once this has been done the case passes out of the hands of the juvenile bureaux and into those of the police officer who will be conducting the case before the court, usually someone from the station to which the child was originally brought. The presentation of the case against a juvenile is never done by the juvenile bureau officer who performed the investigation into the social side.

The full statistics relating to the juvenile bureaux in London show that of the 30,499 children who committed offences in 1972 (a decrease of nearly 5 per cent on 1971) 4,814 were charged immediately on arrival at the police station, 12,106 were summonsed after consideration by the juvenile bureau, 10,516 were cautioned and no further action was taken in 3,013 cases. These proportions, however, differ from area to area, a point to which we return in a later chapter.

Over the country as a whole a total of 82,099 persons under seventeen were cautioned during 1972. 56,835 boys and 15,973 girls were cautioned for indictable offences, and 8,380 boys and 911 girls for non-indictable offences, other than those involving motoring. But a much larger proportion of the children seen by the police ended up in court. In 1972, about 120,000 children were found guilty of both indictable and non-indictable offences by the courts. All but a tiny percentage of these children were dealt with by the juvenile courts.

The procedures described above show up very clearly that in dealing with juveniles, the police are trying to fulfil two roles – a law enforcement one on the one hand and a social policy one on the other. The police remain the authority who take the decision to proceed against a juvenile in court, who prepare the case against him, and who present that case in court. At the same time they have the task of collecting together all the information on the child's social and educational background. They go as far as themselves investigating the child's family and home conditions. Any decision made about them has to balance the demands of the proper administration of justice and the protection of society with the welfare and well-being of the child.

Should the police be made to fulfil this dual function? This is a question to which we return in a later chapter, but a stark illustration of the ambiguity of the police role is provided by the following example given by a senior police officer with considerable experience in the working of the juvenile bureaux. A bureau police constable goes to the home of a petty juvenile offender to conduct a home inquiry. During the course of conversation the child unexpectedly reveals that he has committed other offences, some more serious than the one under consideration. Is the police officer to turn a deaf ear to this confession or is he immediately to change his role, put on his law enforcement hat, caution the child and take a statement?

If he does so, what of the effect this has on the child and his parents, who would, to some extent justifiably, think to themselves that they had been tricked into receiving the policeman into their homes and helping him? It is fair to say that many police officers have some reservations about their role as social workers. They would prefer to remain in their traditional role, but rightly claim that their work in helping young people has been of considerable value to the community.

5 The Magistracy and the Juvenile Courts

The juvenile courts as a separate institution were first established under the Children Act 1908. Up to that time there was in law very little distinction made between juvenile and adult offenders. The only concessions to children had been a trend, starting with an Act passed in 1847, of having the lower courts deal with some offences committed by children which would have been tried by a jury in the higher courts if committed by an adult. The Summary Jurisdiction Act 1879 made more offences triable summarily, so that in fact by the turn of the century most children were dealt with by the magistrates' courts.

But offences, whether by adults or juveniles, were still being dealt with by the same courts at the same hearings. There was no legal or physical separation between children and adults on the day of the trial. At about the turn of the century, however, the practice grew up in certain areas of having court hearings involving juveniles at different times from the other cases. But this was a purely unofficial procedure instituted by some enlightened magistrates with particular interest in and concern for children. They themselves manned these embryo juvenile courts on a rota basis.

A few years later the 1908 Act conferred the force of law on such arrangements. The Act was amended on numerous occasions, until by the Children and Young Persons Act 1933 the juvenile courts were finally properly set up. The juvenile court system of today is with only minor changes still based on the 1933 Act. There are now more than 800 juvenile courts in England and Wales.

One central issue that has preoccupied those concerned in helping children in trouble has been whether these courts are in fact the right places to deal with child offenders. At the turn of the century they were plainly an improvement on the confused legal position of children in the courts, but as the twentieth century, with its growing emphasis on social welfare in a non-legal setting, has progressed, their usefulness and on occasion their very existence has come to be questioned. Their critics point out that they are asked to fulfil now the same dual function, of being both a judicial and a welfare agency, as the police are in the juvenile bureau scheme. We shall return to this issue in a later chapter. For the foreseeable future, however, the juvenile courts will continue to deal with children and it is therefore important to explain their functions.

Beginning with the magistrates themselves, at present nearly half the 21,000-strong magistracy is entitled to sit in the juvenile courts. At the moment they are appointed by a different procedure in London to that which governs the rest of England and Wales. The Lord Chancellor appoints the juvenile magistrates in London, and the Children and Young Persons Act 1969 gave him the power to do so everywhere, but at the time of writing he has not yet exercised this power. Outside London the magistrates of each petty sessional area choose a juvenile panel of magistrates from amongst themselves by election. How many are picked depends in theory on the requirements of the particular area. It is important to remember that no one can sit on the juvenile court bench who is not a magistrate and that all magistrates are appointed by the Lord Chancellor.

Juvenile magistrates must be less than sixty-five years old and any sitting magistrate must retire from the juvenile bench as soon as he reaches that age (although he can continue to sit in the ordinary magistrates court). In practice, however, most magistrates and the Lord Chancellor follow the recommendation of the report of the Commission on Justices of the Peace in 1948 that the most suitable age for a first appointment to the juvenile panel is between thirty and forty and that only in exceptional circumstances should someone over fifty be appointed for the first time. Complying with that recommendation, however, is often difficult. Persons do not often become magistrates before their mid-thirties, more often in their forties. The average age of magistrates is thought to be in the upper forties, and there are just not sufficient magistrates of thirty to forty to be appointed to the juvenile bench, even assuming they fulfil the other requirements laid down.

The principal requirement is that those appointed to the juvenile panel, according to Rules made by the Lord Chancellor under the 1933 Act, must be 'specially qualified' to deal with juvenile cases. No further guidance is officially given as to the interpretation of 'specially qualified'. The departmental Committee on young offenders in 1927, on which the 1933 Act was based, suggested that experience of social work amongst youth would be a valuable asset and obviously someone with professional or academic qualifications concerning the problems of young children would be acceptable. But the number of magistrates with such qualifications would fall short of the number needed to adequately man the juvenile courts. The Departmental Committee went on to suggest that other desirable qualities were 'a love of young people, sympathy with their interests, and an imaginative insight into their difficulties'. It is not surprising that the special suitability for children criterion is interpreted with considerable variations, and the standards and quality of the juvenile panels differ greatly from area to area.

One persistent criticism of all magistrates, not just those sitting on the juvenile bench, is that they are still taken very largely from the professional and upper social classes (recent surveys have put the proportion at more than 75 per cent) whereas the people who tend to appear before them are from the other sections of the community. For juveniles, the issue is whether an affluent middle-class professional man living in a comfortable home can really have the necessary insight into the difficulties faced by the thirteen-year-old boy from a poor, inadequate family living in a deprived area – a situation common to a large proportion of juvenile offenders. Some, of course, do have this insight. Others on the juvenile bench very patently do not have the requisite understanding.

What training do magistrates receive to enable them to better cope with the child offender who appears before them? Training for magistrates generally has been compulsory only since 1966. Magistrates appointed to the juvenile bench have, in addition, to undergo a special course of training which takes the form of lectures by and contacts with experts in the various fields which coping with delinquents involves, as well as visits to the institutions to which the children who appear in their courts might be sent, and sitting in on court hearings.

Another requirement is that there must either be two or three magistrates sitting on a juvenile bench including one of each sex. So if only two sit, it must be a man and a woman (except in unforeseen or emergency circumstances, when two of the same sex may sit, or a stipendiary magistrate may sit alone). The juvenile panel of the area must therefore be chosen with this in mind and this has on occasion conflicted with the 'specially qualified' criteria. Two-thirds of all magistrates, but only 60 per cent of juvenile magistrates, are men. A poor quality woman will often have to be preferred to a higher quality male in order to keep to the sex-representation requirement.

It has been said that, especially outside London, the selection of magistrates for the juvenile panel is 'largely haphazard and sometimes very unsuitable'. This judgement may be overharsh, but it has unfortunately enough truth in it to warrant the criticism sometimes levelled that the fate of our delinquent children is too often entrusted to those who lack the qualities necessary to carry out that trust.

Apart from the quality of the magistrates themselves, a persistent criticism of juvenile courts has revolved round the nature of the premises in which hearings are held and the procedures in the courtroom. The Children and Young Persons Act 1933 expressed the hope that the juvenile court would be in a different building to that of the adult criminal courts. More realistically, it also provided for the alternative of having juvenile court sittings in the same building but on different days from the adult crime courts (and, it was envisaged, in a different room). Even this had to be modified, however, and the Children and Young Persons Act 1963 allowed juvenile courts to be held on the same day and in the same courtroom as adult trials provided there was a gap of an hour between the juvenile and the adult sittings. To achieve the same aim – of seeing to it that child offenders do not have any contact with adult criminals – there are also regulations governing the transportation of children to and from the court and the waiting periods at the court.

It is virtually impossible to make any generalizations about juvenile court premises in use in England and Wales today. In some cases – only a few – a juvenile court is in specially designed premises in a building separate from any other court buildings. At the other extreme, in many areas, proceedings involving juveniles take place in the same courtroom as is used for criminal trials, although usually on a different day. In between the two extremes a variety of arrangements are in use. Some juvenile court hearings are held in the court building but in a different room. Other juvenile courts sit in a room in the local town hall, or other local authority building. It has even been known for a court to sit in a church hall.

Obviously facilities differ greatly in quality and appropriateness, especially in regard to accommodation for children waiting, sometimes for hours, for their cases to come up, with their parents and witnesses. Deficiencies in waiting accommodation has for a long time been the subject of widespread criticism. The layout of the room where the hearings are held also varies widely from court to court, and about this too, there has been much adverse comment. In some cases, the layout is forced on the court by physical factors. For example, where the juvenile court sits in the normal courtroom there is little alternative but to use the room in the usual manner. On the other hand where in effect the court sits in a room which does not impose a particular structure, much can be done to achieve what could be considered a more appropriate layout.

The broad philosophy is that the room in which hearings are held should be so designed as to give the impression that what is taking place is a serious and formal procedure intended to instil some sense of dignity, apprehension and feeling of responsibility into the child and his parents without at the same time so overwhelming and intimidating the child that an unbridgeable gap is created between him and the magistrates.

Under the present procedures, however, even the most enlightened efforts to devise a sympathetic structural layout for the hearing has come up against the difficulty that a comparatively large number of people are entitled to be in the court during the hearing. Because of this it has proved almost impossible to get away from the general layout and atmosphere of an adult criminal court. Those who can be present are: the magistrates, their legally qualified clerk (who administers the hearing and advises the magistrates on the law, procedure and sentencing), another court official, the child, his parents, their legal representatives (if any), witnesses, the police or other prosecutor presenting the case, probation officers, social workers and members of the press. Only the general public is excluded, their interest in open justice being safeguarded by the press. Given this number of persons present, and even though attempts are made to have the magistrates sitting on more or less the same height level as the child appearing before them, the appearance of a trial is unmistakable. This is reinforced by the procedure used, which is equally unmistakeably based, although with modifications, on that of an adult criminal trial.

The procedure is that the charge is put to the juvenile, which he may either admit or deny. If he admits it, the presenting police officer outlines the details of the case. The magistrates are provided with what reports are available on the child's home background and history and sometimes hear oral evidence from the social worker or probation officer. If these are not available the child has to be remanded for two or three weeks whilst the necessary inquiries are made. When they have been given all the relevant information the magistrates usually call the child's parents over to them and discuss the case with them. The parents are then sent back and the magistrates talk to the child himself. After discussing the case among themselves they announce their decision.

If the juvenile does not admit the offence the case is handled in exactly the same manner as a full-scale criminal trial, with examination of witnesses, cross-examination and speeches by the legal representatives (legal aid is usually made available for contested cases). If his guilt is found proved by the magistrates the procedure thereafter is the same as for an admitted offence. (In practice only a tiny minority of children fail to admit having committed the offence with which they have been charged.) A decision of the juvenile court can be taken on appeal to the Crown Court.

Although some attempt is made to simplify the procedure and

terminology so that it can be better understood by the child and his parents, especially if there is no lawyer representing the child, the language is still that of a court of law. How successful the attempt at easier language procedure, and how easy the atmosphere in the court, depends largely on the justices' clerk, although of course the approach of the magistrates themselves is also important.

What are the powers of the magistrates to deal with juveniles who have admitted or have been proved to have committed an offence? Where the child is brought to court under the provisions relating to criminal proceedings, they can grant an absolute or a conditional discharge, or fine the offender, subject to an upper limit of £10 for children under fourteen and £50 for those between fourteen and seventeen. The magistrates can order the parent or guardian to pay that fine. In addition to the fine, the offender or his parent or guardian can be ordered to compensate any victim of the offence for his loss.

They can bind over the offender, or his parents or guardian, but only with their consent. They can make a care order placing the child in the care of the local authority, if the offence is of such gravity as would be punishable by imprisonment if it were committed by an adult. A new power given under the 1969 Act allows them to make a supervision order, which requires the child to be under the supervision of the local authority of the area or the probation service. (The local authority in turn assigns a social worker to establish the relationship with and give support to the offender.)

The magistrates can continue to make for boys, as they could under the old law, an attendance centre order, or, where the child is over fourteen, a detention centre order. These institutions will be described more fully in a later chapter. They can also commit an offender over fifteen to the Crown Court with a recommendation that he be sentenced to borstal. Finally, although this is rarely used, magistrates have the power to make a guardianship order, and place the offender under the guardianship of a particular person or authority, or a hospital order where the offender's mental condition is such that he requires hospital treatment.

Where the child comes before the court under section 1 of the

1969 Act, the provisions relating to care proceedings, magistrates are empowered only to make care, supervision, guardianship or hospital orders, or bind over the parent or guardian to exercise proper control over the child.

In 1972, of the 21,117 boys and girls under fourteen who appeared before the magistrates and were found guilty of indictable offences, an absolute discharge was given to 470 and a conditional discharge to a further 5,723. Supervision orders were made in 5,593 cases, whilst in 2,415 cases the children were placed in the care of the local authority. Fines were imposed on 4,393 offenders, whilst in 2,451 cases attendance centre orders were made.

In 1972 the juvenile courts also made orders for 53,582 boys and girls aged between fourteen and seventeen who came before them and were found guilty of indictable offences. Absolute discharges accounted for 879 offenders and conditional discharges for a further 9,559 boys and girls. A supervision order was made in 9,561 cases and a care order in 3,710. The largest single form of dealing with offenders of this age was again by fining which was imposed on 22,450 occasions. The courts made 1,855 detention centre orders and 3,709 attendance centre orders for boys of fourteen to seventeen. In 1,585 cases of boy offenders and forty-two of girls the magistrates committed them to a higher court with a recommendation for borstal.

More than forty per cent of children under seventeen who came before the courts, therefore, were fined for their offences. Slightly less than a fifth were given discharges, either conditional or absolute, and about the same percentage were placed under supervision. Care orders were made for only about seven per cent of the children appearing before the court. About three fifths of the children brought before the juvenile courts, therefore, are allowed to go home by the magistrates without any further contact with any other authority, and about a quarter are placed under the care or supervision of the local authority social workers or the probation service.

6 Social Workers

Social workers as a breed of men and women are no new phenomenon, although they were not known by that name until comparatively recently. In the nineteenth century they worked for philanthropic institutions, or on their own, or in the reformatory and industrial schools, to help children in trouble. During the twentieth century they continued to do so, in the new, or newly named, institutions, such as the approved schools. They also worked for voluntary bodies helping the children of the poor, the children of the homeless, or children who had been abandoned by their parents.

During the thirties the term social worker first came into common use and in 1948 the Children Act acknowledged them formally in the children's departments of the local authorities. The Act created the children's service for the specific purpose of caring for children who, either permanently or temporarily, were deprived of their home life. In 1963 the Children and Young Persons Act specifically also charged them with trying to prevent children getting into trouble or being brought before the courts.

As the function of the children's departments increased, so did society's awareness of the usefulness of social workers. They offered help, support and sometimes treatment to unhappy, often unloved and unwanted children and they did so outside the context of punishment, the prisons and the police. As consciousness grew that social deprivation created its own diseases – and one of these was children who got into trouble with the law – the important role which could be played by the social worker increased.

The social workers within children's departments fell into three principal categories. There were the administrators, who did not directly deal with problem children and their parents; the officers directly responsible for individual cases who visited homes offering advice and help; and the residential staff in the homes, local authority or voluntary children's approved schools or remand homes.

By 1967 the child care officers in the second category, the workers in the field, had acquired an excellent reputation for helping children of all kinds who got into *any* kind of trouble whether criminal or not. They did not simply concern themselves with offenders, but all kinds of children who were taken – or might be taken – into local authority's care.

So they looked after the children whose mother or father had been temporarily taken ill, illegitimate or abandoned children, as well as those children who appeared in the courts as offenders, and were given to the local authority to care for.

The child care officers' good reputation was based on a wealth of experience and ability, and a dedication to the view that most children in trouble of any kind benefited most from staying with their own family.

Sadly, in the residential homes and schools, however, the reputation of the social workers was not as high – partly a result of the different kind of job they were called on to do. A woman social worker from the local authority who visited a home and talked to a child and its parents was clearly doing a somewhat less demanding job than a social worker who was constantly on call to the often very difficult residents of a home or an approved school, who might well be suffering from severe social problems, and had been sent away from their homes for that very reason. It is also not unfair to point out that the residential institutions used often to attract a comparatively poorer quality of social worker.

Before the Children and Young Persons Act 1969 the children's departments around the country were mainly responsible for – as one report of the Home Office's Children's Department put it –

> acting as the main point of contact with outside agencies and with individuals seeking help; of maintaining central records of families being helped by the various services; of undertaking case work with families in their own homes and supervising individual children on a voluntary basis; and of providing material and financial assistance in suitable cases.

Those children who could not be helped in their own homes

were placed with foster parents where possible and appropriate or they were put into one of the residential establishments run by the local authority.

The size and responsibility of the social workers' task in local authority children's departments can be judged from the statistics. In March 1968, for example, almost 70,000 children were in care, about 30,000 girls and 40,000 boys. They had arrived in care for two principal reasons: a breakdown in their family (16,000 or so were in care because of either the death – or pregnancy – of their mother) or because they had been placed in care by the courts (about 22,000 children including non-offenders came into care this way). Almost half the children coming into care were not of school age, and a very large number of the children remained in care only for a matter of a few weeks.

This pattern of the need for care has not broadly altered. But the shape of the official organization that administers that care has been transformed – and as we argue elsewhere tragically so for children in trouble. In 1965 the Home Secretary, the Ministers for Health and for Housing and Local Government, and the Secretary of State for Education and Science jointly appointed a committee to consider the organization and responsibilities of the local authority social services departments. The committee was a distinguished and influential one, led by Mr Frederic (later Lord) Seebohm.

The reforms that the committee recommended in 1968 were far reaching. They involved submerging the successful children's departments in new social services departments, and advocated that all social workers should in future cover all fields of social welfare. In other words all social workers who had previously dealt with only one area, say geriatrics or mental health or children, would in future be responsible for every kind of social welfare problem. There were no longer to be any specialists.

The reforms became law by the Local Authority Social Services Act 1970, which came into force on 1 January 1971 – exactly the same date as the Children and Young Persons Act 1969.

The coincidence of these two major government reforms, both affecting the way in which the social workers in local authorities and residential institutions coped with children, was to prove extremely unfortunate. Social workers were given more responsibility for caring for children under the 1969 Act, which specifically attempted to give more children in trouble to the social worker for care (rather than the court sending them directly to approved schools, for example). But at the same time, because of the other Act, the social workers themselves were desperately trying to reorganize, and local authorities were being forced to use some people who had previously had very little experience with children to cope with children in trouble.

In some courts after January 1971 it was possible to see angry magistrates confronting a child whom they had placed in care reappearing before them time and time again after committing offences, and the only course effectively open to them under the 1969 Act being to leave the child in the care of the local authority. But that care may have been given to the child by a social worker whose only previous experience had been with geriatrics and with the disabled, and the sight of an angry, aggressive thirteen-year-old who had been convicted of a crime involving violence filled at least some of them with terror.

To judge the range of responsibility given to the social workers – who under the Seebohm reforms, would no longer specialize – it is worth referring to the 1970 Act, a schedule to which lists some of their responsibilities. They include, for example:

Protection of the young in relation to criminal and summary proceedings; children appearing before court as in need of care, protection, or control; committal of children to approved school or care of fit person, etc.

Remand homes, approved schools and children in care of fit persons.

Care of expectant and nursing mothers and young children.

Provision of domestic help for certain households.

Provision of residential accommodation for the aged, infirm, needy, etc.

Welfare of persons who are blind, deaf, dumb or otherwise handicapped or are suffering from mental disorder; use of voluntary organizations for administration of welfare schemes.

Registration of disabled or old persons' homes, residential homes for mentally disordered persons and charities for the disabled.

Provisions for orphans, deserted children; children suffering from mental disorder, etc.; assumption by local authority of parental rights; local authority as a fit person under the Act of 1933; children in care; financing of children's maintenance and education, etc.; registration of voluntary children's homes and use of voluntary organizations.

Regulation of nurseries and child minders.

Making, etc., arrangements for the adoption of children; regulation of adoption societies; care, possession and supervision of children awaiting adoption; prosecution of offences.

Supervision of wards of court.

None of these responsibilities was new to social workers, as a whole. What was distinctly new, however, was the way they were organized to carry them out. The Local Authority Social Services Act 1970 specifically called upon local authorities to appoint a director of social services to direct all the operations of social workers. When this happened the social workers themselves tended to be re-grouped into teams. Every member of a team of social workers would probably have had experience in one of the areas for which they were responsible, but each one might have to do anything.

This 'generic' approach to social workers' jobs has much to commend it. It means that within any team of workers there is all the available expertise it may need to call on for any single case. But the approach did mean that in the short run many social workers who had to try and help children who got into trouble had no previous experience whatsoever with them.

This reorganization of the way they did their jobs took place, as we have said, at exactly the same time as they were receiving greater responsibilities for children under the terms of the Children and Young Persons Act 1969. This meant that social workers were doubly handicapped. Indeed, Sir Keith Joseph, the Secretary of State for Health and Social Security, admitted early in 1973 that the Government had been mistaken in implementing these two major changes at the same time. Sir Keith said, 'We are trying to do a great number of new things at the same time, trying to catch up on many neglected sectors of the social services', and he went on, 'We should not have done it all at once.'

It is difficult to see, however, how the Government could have done anything else. People involved in both areas had been in the centre of controversy and speculation for almost a decade and once a decision to reform them had been taken it was almost impossible to halt the momentum which had built up by postponing one or other of the reforms.

The reorganization emphasized the fact that only about 40 per cent of the 9,000 or so social workers who were then employed by the local authorities had any real training or experience in dealing with children, and the number of children coming into care was rising rapidly. On 31 March 1970 there were 68,255 children in the care of local authorities, but by one year later (including the first few months of the 1969 Act's operations) this number had risen dramatically to 83,621.

This put the stretched social workers under considerable pressure. For although there is no clear estimate of how many social workers are necessary to carry out all the functions expected of them – including the increased responsibilities for children – it would seem fair to estimate on the basis that there are now almost 11,000 social workers in England and Wales, that they are between 2,000 and 3,000 persons short.

For children in trouble, however, there is one further crucial complication in their receiving the help and treatment the 1969 Act envisages – disagreement about how it should be given. In simple terms some sections of society believe that punishment and discipline is still of great importance in dealing with a child who gets into trouble with the law, while others believe that any crime a child may have committed is simply the expression of his physical, emotional or environmental deprivation and that he needs care and help to overcome those deprivations and to cease to commit offences.

Clearly these two views are not necessarily exclusive, nor are they held by everyone – many people believe, for example, that a little of both approaches is the best system for children in trouble. But the 1969 Act was really an expression of the second belief and an attempt to give it legislative existence. The Act's supporters saw more than 3,000 social workers in children's departments doing an excellent job in helping children in trouble and aimed to increase the part they played in helping all children. They also saw the residential institutions, and particularly the approved schools, doing what they felt was a less than adequate job (although we believe this was unfair) and wanted to have more centralized control over the part they were playing.

But the Act did something else. It curtailed the powers which were believed to be necessary by those who felt that punishment and discipline were a key part of the answer to juvenile delinquency. Many of that group were to be found among magistrates, and the Act, therefore, unwittingly set up a clash in the juvenile courts. For the two views, although not held rigidly by every member of either side, tended to confront each other there. The magistrates were now less powerful – they could not send a child to an approved school – and resented this loss of power. They could now only put the child into the care of a local authority, with a recommendation for residential care (which the social workers could and did ignore). Contact, understanding and trust between the courts and social services lessened considerably.

This confrontation accounted for many of the difficulties that the Act encountered when it came into operation. The magistrates felt that children were not being disciplined sufficiently – and to prove it they could instance a worryingly large number of children in care committing offences over and over again with no fear of punishment. On the other hand the social workers, who were dedicated to helping children in a less obviously punitive way, and had been called upon to do so very firmly by the 1961 Act, found themselves in turmoil because of their reorganization. We return to these difficulties in a later chapter.

One group of social workers who do not fall into the main categories described above, but who operate in both the juvenile and adult courts are probation officers, of whom there were, in September 1973, 4,381 in England and Wales. Originally the 1969 Act intended that they should confine their work to the adult courts, where they had been of great help and had gained enormous respect over the years. In the end, however, the juvenile courts were allowed, when making a supervision order on a juvenile, to make a probation officer responsible for that supervision. It was envisaged that this could be done, for instance, where the probation officer already knew and was working with the family to which the young offender belonged.

This was partly an acknowledgement on the part of the

Government of the difficulties that the local authority social workers were facing in their job. The inexperience of some of them, both as a result of their transfer from other areas and their youth, made both Government and magistrates reticent about giving them complete responsibility for all children. There was therefore a curious compromise. The old probation order was done away with, and a new form of supervision order was put in its place. Supervision of a child could still be given to probation officers, although in due course (when the local authorities had worked out some of their difficulties) they would handle fewer and fewer supervision cases.

One general implication of the 1969 Act was also that local authority social workers should have more responsibility for and control over more institutions to which children in trouble could be sent.

7 Institutions, Punishment and Therapy

The variety of places in which children under seventeen who get into trouble can find themselves is vast, and the different kinds of régime to which they may become subject is even more so. The institutions range from small homes with a family atmosphere to large borstals or even prisons, and the régimes from the informal and loving to the disciplinarian and punitive. What follows is a guide to the principal institutions to which juvenile offenders may be sent.

The approved schools were brought into the community homes system by the 1969 Act, but it is convenient to discuss them as a separate entity. Their name may have changed, but their characteristics often have not.

The name came from the approval given to them by the Secretary of State for the Home Department under the terms of the Children and Young Persons Act 1933, which created these schools from the existing reformatories and industrial schools. Before the 1969 Act thirty of the 126 schools were managed by local authorities and the rest were independent schools managed by religious bodies or voluntary groups, such as Dr Barnardo's and the Salvation Army. Now, under the terms of the 1969 Act, they are all to be run by the local authority as one of a number of residential institutions known as community homes, including former children's homes and hostels. (This change was partly the result of the criticism that had been levelled against the schools, particularly during the sixties.)

The approved schools can never be described simply. They are all 'open' institutions, in that the boys or girls who go to them are subject to rules and discipline, but not to any kind of physical restraint from leaving. The youngest a child theoretically could go to an approved school was ten. The oldest was, again theoretically, seventeen, although more often it was eighteen in practice.

Children were not sent to the schools for a fixed term, but rather for a period of education and training. In practice during the middle sixties boys tended to stay in the schools for an average of twenty months, and girls for an average of seventeen months, although the older boys and girls tended to stay longer. It was possible under the system governing the schools before the 1969 Act for a child to spend up to six years in the schools, but this was extremely rare.

The 126 schools, ninety-one of them for boys and the rest for girls, could accept children the courts found guilty of offences, or who were in need of care, or indeed had been found guilty of truancy. As much as a sixth of the population could consist of non-offenders. At their peak they housed about 8,000 boys and girls, although by April 1972 their population had fallen to just under 6,000 (about 5,000 boys and 900 girls). Since then there has been a gradual rise and on 31 March 1973 there were 6,557 boys and girls in the schools.

Four of the boys' schools, Aycliffe in Durham, Kingswood in Bristol, Red Bank at Newton-le-Willows and Redhill in Surrey, acted as classifying centres for all the schools. These schools were responsible for building up by observation and investigation a picture of the child's history, background and, as the Home Office put it, his or her 'needs and potentialities'. The child could then be allocated to the most suitable approved school and those who were helping him were provided with some information on which to base their approach. There was also some classifying done at Stamford House remand home for boys in London, while girls – for whom there was no classifying approved school – were either observed and assessed in London or in Sheffield at special classifying centres. (Boys of course made up by far the major proportion of the schools' population.)

Approved schools generally had a dismal record for dissuading young people from committing further offences. In 1964, for example, 3,884 boys were released from the schools and 2,647 of them committed further offences within three years – 68 per cent. In the same year 732 girls were released and 156 committed further offences within three years – 21 per cent.

Part of the reason for the lack of success may have been that the more 'criminal' children sometimes corrupted the less delinquent, and even the non-offenders. In any event, as has been remarked by more than one expert, the approved schools seemed to have been largely counter-productive. They were also comparatively expensive. Before the 1969 Act, it cost more than £23 a week to keep a boy at the schools. Today, this amount would have risen appreciably. The staff, although they were paid in excess of the Burnham scale for teachers, were often untrained in social work, and were also difficult to find. The traditional approved-school master was more often a former military man than a graduate, more used to the drill of the parade ground than the therapeutic theories that were gaining ground during the sixties.

Mr W. David Wills points out in *Spare the Child*, his book on one of the most adventurous and respected approved schools, the Cotswold Community run by Mr Richard Balbernie:

> It is difficult as well as rash to make generalizations about some 120 schools dealing with about 8,000 children whose ages range from ten to eighteen and whose intelligence varies as greatly as their ages. It must be borne in mind, moreover, that the schools are not part of a unified state system like prison and borstal; each one, though subject to Home Office rules and to inspection by Home Office inspectors, is a separate independent unit . . . some of them take a more punitive attitude than others, some incline towards a more therapeutic approach.

One characteristic of the approved schools in the sixties was that many seemed rooted firmly in the past. They still showed many signs of the view that a boy or girl in trouble was somehow morally depraved and was therefore in the institution for punishment. Many excellent residential workers fought hard against this prevailing conception, and some of the best schools triumphantly escaped from it, but nevertheless this tended to give the approved schools a distinctly Victorian punitive flavour.

It was very much this flavour, coupled with three unfortunate and much-publicized cases – the murder of a master at Standom Farm in 1947, a mass break-out and quasi-riot at Carlton House in 1959 and the canings at Court Lees in 1967 – that led to the firm belief among liberals that these institutions should be abolished in their existing forms. It was mainly with the small independent schools in mind, those run by voluntary bodies in an old-fashioned way, that the provisions of the 1969 Act were drafted (although it is fair to say that some of the independent schools were very good indeed).

It is, as we have pointed out, almost impossible to describe a 'typical' approved school. The more modern ones have tended to be built in separate small units, each housing a maximum of thirty children in relatively cheerful conditions – in sharp contrast to the austerity of the older buildings with their large depressing dormitories. Approved schools resemble ordinary boarding schools in many ways, including having a similar staff structure with headmaster, housemasters and teachers in various subjects in the curriculum.

In some cases children go to the local schools in the nearest centres of population, but most are educated at the approved school itself. Classes there, however, tend to be smaller than those in ordinary schools and more concerned with remedial work, as many of the pupils suffer from considerable educational neglect. As they approach school-leaving age the children are given more vocationally orientated training, and will spend an increasing amount of their time in the school's workshop or craftroom. Arrangements have been made so that in some trades training at an approved school can count as part of the apprenticeship period.

More emphasis is now being placed on providing pupils with a 'social' education as well – getting on with other people and in the society to which they will eventually return. Many schools, for instance, have schemes for fostering contact between the children and the local community. Outside of school hours, leisure activities are usually well catered for, with facilities for many games and sports.

Approved schools, other than those catering for special needs, have not been built with security in mind. There are no high walls and barbed wire. But inside the schools discipline is strict. Most schools run some system of rewards and privileges – such as extra pocket money – for good behaviour. But relatively minor infringements of the school's rules can be punished by relatively severe penalties, such as fines, deprivation of home leave, and withdrawal of the right to watch television (which in a residential home can be a very real deprivation). In exceptional circumstances corporal punishment can still be applied.

Ultimately, however, whatever the facilities, the success or failure of an approved school may depend on the personality of the staff, and particularly that of its headmaster or headmistress. Experience has shown that the quality of staff is a more important factor in assessing an approved school's achievement than any physical conditions. Some of the most inspired and inspiring leadership and guidance has emerged from the shabbiest surroundings, whilst modern model schools have failed because their staff has been unable to strike up the necessary relationships with the children.

In reality the approved schools were much better than their public image may have led the outsider to believe. Some boys and girls drew profound benefit and support from them, but their statistical results in discouraging young people from further crime did not persuade the legislators and others that they should continue to exist in their present form. Indeed, the often dilapidated condition of their buildings, some of them old and cramped Victorian houses deep in the countryside, showed how much they had been ignored and looked down upon for three decades. Only a few local authority run schools seemed to escape this opprobrium.

Although the schools were conceived and designed largely as 'open' institutions there was a move in the sixties to provide three specially secure units for boys who persistently ran away or were exceptionally difficult. These three units, which housed seventy-six boys, were built at three of the classifying schools during the sixties. One of them, at Red Bank in Newton-le-Willows, was subsequently adapted to house one girl, Mary Bell, the eleven-year-old girl convicted of the murder of two other children. After the 1969 Act came into force ten further smaller secure units were added in the schools, which could house fifty-one boys or girls. All the specially secure units at the schools have almost always been full.

Remand homes were boarding institutions provided by the local authorities under the Children and Young Persons Act,

1933. The cost of maintaining them was met jointly by the local authorities and the central government.

They are also now part of the community homes system. There were some sixty of them before the 1969 Act came into force, providing places for more than 1,500 boys and girls who were remanded without bail and were awaiting a court appearance. The children in the homes may have been charged with offences or may have been before the courts as in need of care, protection or control. They also provided 'safe custody' – a phrase which was constantly applied about them for boys and girls waiting for a vacancy in an approved school.

Of the sixty homes, all but two were run by local authorities singly or jointly and all but three were single-sex. There were twenty-three girls' homes and thirty-four boys' homes. In the sixties the boys' homes were generally about 80 per cent full and the girls' homes 70 per cent full. The average length of stay for both was just over three weeks although towards the end of the sixties girls tended to stay in the homes slightly longer.

Five of the remand homes were categorized as classifying centres under the Children and Young Persons Act 1963. These helped decide what form of treatment was best for children that passed through them. Reports were prepared by the staff for use by the courts.

Because children sent to a remand home are supposed to remain there for a period of weeks only (although unfortunately in some cases this stretches into months), facilities in these homes are necessarily limited. Nevertheless attempts are made to see to it that the children's schooling does not suffer overmuch. In the words of the Home Office booklet, *The Sentence of the Court*,

> in most remand homes, education for children of school age is designed to minimize the disadvantages of an interruption of schooling; older boys and girls receive training in practical subjects, such as woodwork, light craftwork, gardening, housecraft and needlework. There is physical recreation and as much as possible is done to encourage the right use of leisure time.

For reasons we go into later, the reality often does not measure up to these good intentions.

Remand homes have more security arrangements than do approved schools, because the children on remand tend to be those most likely to commit further offences if free. They have often been refused bail for that very reason. Discipline is harsh, on the whole, and without the sophistication found in many approved schools. More emphasis is placed on locking up than on mere withdrawal of privileges. Many remand homes have special secure rooms in which a recalcitrant child can be kept in isolation. Although leisure facilities exist, the nature of the homes inevitably results in these being less elaborate than in the approved schools, where children may spend years. It is again difficult to talk of 'typical' remand home conditions. Some homes, for instance, are converted private homes, where there would only be a few children to a room. Others have large dormitories. One significant point of difference between remand homes and approved schools is that in the former there is virtually no chance for a relationship to develop between staff and children. The atmosphere is therefore far more formal.

The remand homes provided one of the finest assessment systems available in the pre-1969 Act period. The staff was generally younger and better trained than the residential staff of the approved schools. This was principally because they were able to work in the remand homes while remaining non-residential. These homes benefited considerably from this. But again, the buildings themselves were often old and dilapidated.

In January 1973 Sir Keith Joseph gave details of an expansion programme for accommodating young offenders both for observation and in remand and longer-stay homes. This was to include an increase in the number of secure places. In October 1973 he gave the latest estimate of this programme. He said that by the end of 1978 there would be secure places for 216 children in 40 new short-term units and another 194 secure places in 14 new long-stay units.

The Labour Government had also decided before the 1969 Act passed through Parliament to build three special youth treatment centres designed to provide security, support and treatment for the most severely disturbed children in trouble. Feeling it would be unfair to make the local authorities responsible for them it took full responsibility itself. They were extremely slow, however, in getting off the ground. The first institution at Brentwood in Essex was built partly under the impetus of Mary Bell's case (although she was not subsequently sent there) and it first opened its doors to six children in July 1971. It closed again shortly afterwards, however, partly because it was not secure enough to persuade the inhabitants to remain in it. It only re-opened again, to five young people, in February 1973. The number of residents is rising slowly and in due course it is designed to house thirty-eight boys and girls, twelve under especially secure conditions.

The two other centres, in Birmingham and Wakefield, are planned to be completed by 1975. They should provide a further 140 places for these severely disturbed children.

The normal age of admission to the centres will be twelve. The maximum age for any resident is likely to be nineteen, although as they are intended to provide long-term treatment the Department of Health and Social Security have suggested that no one over sixteen should be admitted. They will not only take the most disturbed children who are in the care of a local authority, but may also house some boys and girls convicted of particularly grave crimes. The juvenile courts will be unable to commit offenders to them directly, and no child is likely to be sent to one of the centres before some other form of residential care has been tried.

One new form of treatment created by the 1969 Act has begun operation in some areas. It is designed to be part of the supervision process, and is aimed at giving the child a range of possible activities – some of them away from home – which would help his or her rehabilitation. Examples of these 'intermediate' forms of treatment include anything from weekly attendance at the local youth club to two or three months at an outward bound course or adventure farm. The choice of activity is to be left to the supervisor, who will make the necessary arrangements.

One of the aims of 'intermediate' treatment is to integrate the offender with the community by allowing him to mix freely with other children of his own age. It is expected that by the middle of

1974 seven of the twelve regional areas in England and Wales will have made arrangements for these many alternative activities to be available where the supervisor feels they would be in the interests of the child.

All the forms of institutions dealt with above – approved schools, remand homes and youth treatment centres – are governed by the local authorities or the DHSS. They are not part of the prison system. A number of other institutions for children in trouble are under the control of the Home Office. These are attendance centres, detention centres and borstals.

Attendance centres are the principal non-residential institutions provided for boys in trouble. They existed before the 1969 Act, being first brought into operation by the Criminal Justice Act 1948. They are controlled by the Home Office, and were originally for twelve- to twenty-one-year-olds, but in 1961 ten-year-olds were allowed to go to them. (In practice there are only two centres for young people over seventeen, in Manchester and Greenwich, London.) They are only to be found in cities and big conurbations.

Most of the sixty-three attendance centres are held in schools, youth clubs or police halls. There is no security around the centre. The child simply has to attend, usually for a minimum of twelve hours and a maximum of twenty-four hours. The centre is normally open for two hours on a Saturday afternoon and a child attends every other week.

In 1972, 6,785 children were sent to these centres by the courts, who tend to use them for younger children who commit a number of offences. They have used them persistently, for example, for vandalism and for hooliganism (although about 60 per cent of the children sent to them had been convicted of breaking and entering or stealing). About fifty-three of the centres concentrate principally on younger children, for whom the order to attend is usually the first time the court has tried some form of deterrent disciplinary treatment. They represent an effort to stop a child who has committed offences from going on to commit even more. The centres were not designed for disturbed children or for those who needed special help, care and support in their own homes, or for those children who already have an established record of offences.

The centres are usually run by retired police officers, or by active off-duty officers. The afternoon's activities start with a period of physical exercise, such as press-ups, and go on to 'leisure' activities, like handicrafts or a lecture. There is a firm emphasis on abiding by the rules and on actual attendance – failure to do so may mean the child is brought back to court for the original offence.

They were designed, according to the Home Office,

> to vindicate the law by imposing loss of leisure, a punishment that is readily understood by children; to bring the offender for a period under the influence of representatives of the state; and, by teaching him something of the constructive use of leisure to guide him on leaving the centres.

They have not been a success. The centres have failed to dissuade children in trouble from committing further offences, they have offered little effective training, and, as far as it is possible to tell, they are held in contempt by the children who attend.

It is important to remember, however, that the centres appear to be greatly liked by the general public and the magistrates, who feel that the concept of punishment that they embody is all too often missing in the modern treatment of children. And they do at least keep some football hooligans off the terraces on match-days.

Detention centres are run by the Prison Department of the Home Office with a staff of warders and a warden appointed from the same grade as prison governors. There are eighteen centres altogether in England and Wales, all of them for boys, but only five of them take children under seventeen. These five institutions, one of which was only recently converted (at Whatton, Nottinghamshire) can house 2,600 boys in a year. In fact, in 1972 2,513 boys were sent to them.

They were set up under the Criminal Justice Act 1948 and the Criminal Justice Act 1961 enabled the juvenile courts to order an offender aged fourteen or over to attend. They are for children who have committed crimes which would be punishable by imprisonment if they were committed by an adult, and are not designed for those children who have already been to borstal. They were designed to give a 'short, sharp shock' and a taste of firm discipline to children who seemed to be starting to commit offences regularly.

They provide full-time education for everyone under sixteen and there are evening classes for the others. There is a lot of emphasis in the régime on physical exercise and there is a considerable amount of para-military drilling in some of the camps. The residents are left very little free time.

Boys under seventeen in almost all cases serve a period of three months' detention with a one-month remission possible for good behaviour (in practice most children who go to the centres get this – probably because they see the centre as only a short-term punishment to be borne with equanimity).

The detention centres have been persistently attacked in the past for being uncreative forms of treatment and indeed one of the objectives of the reform movement during the sixties – clearly expressed in *The Child, the Family and the Young Offender* – was that they should cease to exist.

In practice the 1969 Act did not directly abolish them for under-seventeens but gave the Government the right to do so. The Conservative Government had 'reserved its position' on this (as it has also done on allowing children under seventeen to go to an attendance centre or borstal). After the 1969 Act came into operation, magistrates began to use these junior detention centres even more intensively than they had done in the past. In 1967 the average number of residents in the centres at any one time was 267, by 1971 it was more than 330 and in 1972 – with a new centre added – it was up to 400. The reason for this increase was simple. The junior detention centre presented the juvenile courts with the only possible penal institution to which they could send a persistently offending boy. They used them as the principal weapon to fight what they saw as a virtual juvenile crime wave which allowed young people to commit crime with impunity. The junior detention centres rapidly increased their population, particularly of fourteen-year-olds and those of fifteen whom the juvenile courts either could not or would not send to borstals.

More than 1,000 children under seventeen were sent to Borstal in 1972 – almost double the figure for 1967. The borstals are the most penal of all the institutions available for children in trouble, for although their régime was originally designed, and does include, some training, the atmosphere and organization of many of them makes them uncannily like prisons.

Borstals began their life in 1900, when the first institution was opened with eight young prisoners at Bedford Prison as an experiment. It moved in 1901 to the village of Borstal near Rochester in Kent (the village thus giving a name to the system). They were incorporated into the law in 1908. A person who had attained the age of fifteen but not twenty-one could be sent there, only by an assize court or quarter sessions judge, not by a magistrate, if he or she was convicted of a crime punishable by imprisonment. Today magistrates still cannot make an order for borstal. They can only, if the child is over fifteen, commit him to the Crown Court with a recommendation for borstal.

There are twenty-three borstals in England and Wales for boys and four for girls, and they are of three main kinds – 'maximum security', 'medium security', and 'open'. None of the borstals, however, is designed to keep the inhabitants within their four walls every hour of the day and night. All allow outside working parties, for example. The length of time spent there is indeterminate – a period of training of not less than six months nor more than two years. A child is released from a borstal when the governor so decides and in practice this tends to be after between nine and fifteen months. In the middle sixties boys tended to stay in borstal for about an average of fifteen months, while girls stayed there on average only about a year.

Before a child is allocated to a borstal, however, he may have to spend a period of time in a conventional prison waiting to get a place, or while the Prison Service decides which is the right borstal for him to be allocated to. He may also be remanded in custody while he is waiting to be brought before the Crown Court judge for sentence to borstal and then spend time in the borstal allocation wing of Manchester Prison, Wormwood Scrubs in London or Holloway in London (in the case of girls waiting to be assessed). All this is common practice in spite of the words of the Criminal Justice Acts that no child under the age of seventeen should be imprisoned.

At the allocation centre in Wormwood Scrubs, for example, three young men often have to share a cramped, cold and outdated cell, and are locked in these cells for long periods of the day and night. These conditions are little different from those which adults face in prison. It has been persistently suggested to us that magistrates in recommending boys for a period of borstal training are aware that the child may spend up to three or four months in conventional prison surroundings and use this as an additional punishment.

The success of the borstals in persuading young people not to commit further offences has again been low. First offenders are seldom sent there and rarely does a period in borstal dissuade a young offender who has already been a delinquent for some years from committing further offences.

Since 1948 the Home Secretary has had the right to build special remand centres for the detention of young people who are fourteen but not yet twenty-one and who are remanded for trial or are awaiting sentence by the courts. A remand centre is designed to provide both secure conditions and opportunities for observation of the residents.

In reality it was thirteen years before the first of the nine existing remand centres – which were supposed to help ensure that children were not remanded to the adult prisons – was built at Ashford in Middlesex in 1961. It can accommodate 1,300 under-twenty-ones. Ordinarily a child under seventeen will not be remanded to the centres, which are again run by the Home Office's Prison Department, but will go to a remand home – now a community home. It is certainly in his best interests that he should do so.

The remand centres have acquired an extremely unpleasant reputation as punitive penal establishments hampered both by lack of staff and lack of resources. All nine centres deal with boys, although three deal with girls as well.

It is worth remembering that about 12 per cent of all young men in custody at any one time are on remand and only a small proportion of these will subsequently be placed in custody. It is clearly fair, therefore, that their remand should be in reasonable conditions, and certainly not in conditions which bear a remarkable resemblance to some of the worst prisons. In fact, some children under seventeen still go to prison.

At a special one-day conference held by the Magistrates Association in January 1973, Sir Keith Joseph, the Secretary of State for Health and Social Security, explained that because he was increasing the number of secure places in the community home system (the three secure units in the approved schools) from seventy-six to 150 he hoped that no children aged fifteen would find themselves in prison. (He did not explain what would happen to the fifteen-year-olds sentenced to borstal by the Crown Court and who would normally be allocated to a borstal from an allocation wing in a prison.)

There are no available statistics for exactly how many children under seventeen are in prison, although Sir Keith explained to the magistrates that they would have to reconcile themselves to the fact that some sixteen-year-olds would continue to go there in spite of the clear philosophy of the Criminal Justice Acts and, of course, the Children and Young Persons Act 1969, that no child under seventeen should find himself in prison.

One way in which a child under seventeen may find himself in prison is by the provision giving magistrates the power, under section 23(2) of the 1969 Act, to classify a young person whom they believe is 'of so unruly a character that he cannot safely be committed to the care of a local authority'. A child certified under this section goes to a secure institution, which is usually prison or a remand centre. In 1971 no fewer than 2,040 children under seventeen were committed to these institutions under this provision, 25 per cent more than in the previous year. In 1972 the figure remained at more than 2,000.

A particularly disturbing aspect of the imprisonment of children has shown itself in recent months with the incarceration of girls as young as fourteen on remand in Holloway women's prison in London, because of a lack of other secure accomoda-tion for 'unruly girls'.

There are also rare circumstances under which a child under seventeen may find himself actually sentenced to a period in prison. First, if he is convicted of murder and detained during Her Majesty's pleasure then he may well find himself in prison.

Secondly, if a person under seventeen is convicted of an offence which would have led to imprisonment for an adult of fourteen years or more then he may be sentenced to be detained 'in such a place and under such conditions' as the Home Secretary may direct. The 'place' may be a prison. (In practice both kinds of offenders may begin their detention in a young prisoners' wing of an adult prison, usually reserved for persons between seventeen and twenty-one.)

8 'A Blank Cheque?' The 1969 Act in Practice: Magistrates' Criticisms

The Children and Young Persons Act 1969 was the culmination of the philosophy that had gathered force during the twentieth century that children in trouble might be the victim of emotional, environmental or physical deprivation and in need of care, protection and love rather than discipline and punishment. The Act set out, within the framework of the English legal system, to provide the machinery which would enable a child's needs to be expertly assessed and adequately met. But for a large number of juvenile offenders the Act went tragically wrong.

The majority of those involved in the Act's operation since its coming into force in January 1971 now believe that it has failed to offer the help, support and treatment it envisaged. Indeed some believe that children in trouble today are no better off than they were before the Act came into effect. Professor Winifred Cavenagh, a former chairman of the Birmingham Juvenile Magistrates Bench and a distinguished academic social scientist, told a gathering of magistrates, social workers and government officials in 1973 that the position then was much worse than before the Act. 'Many reform and rehabilitation facilities which should be provided by the State were on paper only. The sanctions which the community looked to the juvenile court to supply appeared to be non-existent.' This view is by no means confined to a small minority.

How fair is this assessment? It is difficult to judge from the published official statistics and studies how the 1969 Act is working in practice. There have been strikingly few studies in any depth of this whole area. The only official research consists of two surveys conducted by the Social Work Service of the Department of Health and Social Security (which took over governmental responsibility for children from the Home Office when the Act came into effect).

The first, published in July 1972 but covering only the first year of the working of the Act, came to the conclusion that in spite of difficulties the Act was working well, even at that early stage. This conclusion was greeted with considerable scepticism from many quarters. But in January 1973 Sir Keith Joseph, the Secretary of State for the Department of Health and Social Security, reiterated the official confidence in the Act's operation. Despite teething troubles, he said, it had set in train the developments that were needed. This official attitude has been bitterly criticized as 'complacent'. The Social Work Service's second survey, published in the middle of 1973, reached broadly similar conclusions to the first.

After talking over a period of several months to a large number of people who work with the Act every day and see its shortcomings at first hand, we are convinced that although it may have had the most laudable objective to offer children in trouble help and care – particularly those most in need – in reality it is offering children not much better treatment than they were given a quarter of a century ago.

Why has this happened? In this section we try to outline the main criticisms which have been made of the Act's working by government officials, magistrates, social workers, police, administrators and those working in the residential homes and schools for children.

One of the most serious general accusations levelled against the way the Act is operating at present is that children under the age of seventeen are now able to commit almost any kind of crime with impunity. The law has, as a result, been made almost irrelevant and an object of mockery among young offenders.

The reason for this is said by juvenile court magistrates to be the taking away of their power by the 1969 Act to make an order to send a child to an approved school. Many children who should be in a residential institution are left free to commit further offences, because, the magistrates allege, the only order the court can now effectively make is one placing the child into the care of the local authority.

Magistrates claim that the 'soft' approach of the social services departments of the local authorities means that children who have committed offences and would have before the Act been sent to approved schools are being sent back instead to their own homes, and their old environment, where they continue to present a potential danger to society by committing further offences. Even where the local authority sent the child to a residential home, they go on, he was able to run away with ease and commit further offences with no fear of any more severe action being taken against him.

To substantiate their allegations the magistrates have produced and circulated to the Government, Members of Parliament and local authorities a dossier of examples of children who have persistently committed offences and have been let off, as they say, 'scot-free'. They allege these children have neither been deterred from offending again by the law nor by the local authority, nor had they received the help envisaged for them by the Act.

One case cited, for example, was of a boy from a broken home in the south of England who first appeared before the juvenile court at the age of twelve, in November 1970. At that time he was placed on probation and an attendance centre order for twelve hours was made. Five months later, in April 1971 (after the Act had come into operation), he appeared again in court on two charges of robbery and six of burglary and he was placed in the care of the local authority. Three months later, in July 1971, he came before the court again on a charge of burglary and asked for eight similar cases to be taken into consideration. The magistrates decided to allow the care order made in April to continue. In October 1971 he came before the court again, this time for causing actual bodily harm, and the magistrates again allowed the care order to continue. Two months later, in December, he was sent to a junior detention centre for three months for burglary, as by then he was fourteen and eligible to go there under law. Not long after his release, in May 1972, he came before the court again and another care order was made. At this stage the local authority found a place for him in a community home. Within a matter of weeks he had failed to return to the home after a week-end visit to his own home. He was found by the police, but he ran away again before he could be returned to the community home. He was found again and again ran away.

In June 1972 he was found for a third time and came before the juvenile court for stealing a bicycle. The magistrates remanded him for a period of one week to the same community home, but he ran away after only being there half an hour. When he was finally found he was remanded by the magistrates to Ashford Remand Centre. In September 1972 he appeared before the bench again charged with theft. The chairman of the juvenile bench which had dealt with him remarked at the annual conference of the Magistrates Association that 'The court was in the ludicrous position that the worse a boy's behaviour – and sometimes it was indeed criminal – the less was it possible to deal with him for his own benefit.'

Another example concerns a thirteen-year-old boy who appeared before the juvenile court in August 1972 on four charges of theft and the like and one of driving under age. The magistrates placed him in the care of the local authority. On 27 November 1972 he appeared again charged with theft and was remanded until 1 December 1972, and then remanded again to the care of the local authority until 8 December. When he finally appeared before the court again on that date he was charged with three further offences of burglary, one of which had been committed on the third of that month, while he was not only in the local authority's care but had been specifically remanded to their care only two days before. He pleaded guilty to all four offences, and asked the court to take eleven others into consideration – all of which had been committed between September and November 1972 when he was in the care of the local authority. The magistrates made attendance centre orders for the boy. Only three days later, on 11 December 1972, the boy was again brought before the juvenile court, pleading guilty to a burglary committed the previous day. He was remanded to the care of the local authority, and was on this occasion sent to a remand home.

Yet another case is that of a boy first placed in the local authority's care at the age of fourteen in July 1971. In April 1972 he was fined for taking a motor car without consent and he was fined again the following month for a similar offence. On 13 June 1972 an attendance centre order was made on him for an offence of causing actual bodily harm. Two weeks later, on 29

June, he appeared again before the court and this time pleaded guilty to five charges of dishonesty – being equipped for theft, stealing seven keys, taking a car without consent, stealing car keys and being equipped for theft, having eighteen keys in his possession. He asked for fifty-seven cases to be taken into consideration, all of them committed during the period between January and June 1972 when he was in the care of the local authority. He was once again placed into care by the magistrates.

Similar examples can be found in almost every area of England and Wales. A senior magistrate from the Midlands, for instance, told of the case of a boy of thirteen placed in care for burglary who ran away no less than sixteen times and had been arrested on other charges after committing a hundred offences during his latest period of freedom. After being returned to care he absconded again. In another case a boy allowed home for the week-end by the local authority, in whose care he had been placed, committed fifty-two further offences during the week-end.

One magistrates' clerk summed up how he saw the situation:

The result is, that those young offenders who commit a very large part of the total crime committed are coming into the juvenile court charged with burglary, theft and violence on a major scale, and the only powers available to the court are to remand or to commit to the care of the local authority, where one finds to one's surprise that they are often not kept in any secure accommodation but are allowed to go home, or kept in accommodation which being insecure results in immediate absconsion, when further offences are committed.

It is not too much to say that a blank cheque has been written for all children and young persons under the age of fifteen, and that there is no effective measure of control over them.

He concluded,

This all tends to contribute to a fast-approaching state of anarchy and the public seems totally unable to protect itself. The courts are impotent, the police seem dazed and the local authority social workers appear to relish their new-found power to over-rule the so-called reactionary ideas of the magistracy.

The magistrates' criticisms can be divided into two broad categories. The first relates to the conduct of the local authority social services departments. The magistrates allege that these departments' tendency to allow some young offenders to return to their own homes after they have been found guilty of serious offences (and where the child appeared to need more intensive, and possibly residential, care) fundamentally undermined public confidence in our system of dealing with children in trouble. They add that it also dangerously diminishes children's respect for the law and for the courts. Finally, they suggest that this cripples the objective of the 1969 Act, which was to gear the treatment and care available to the needs of the children.

The second leg of the magistrates' criticism is aimed at the Government and the local authorities' failure to provide enough accommodation, and particularly secure accommodation, for children in trouble. They appreciate that in many of the cases where children in care are returned to their own homes, the local authority had attempted to find a more suitable, and possibly secure, place to send them, but had been unable to do so. Without these facilities the magistrates appreciate that both they and the local authorities are prevented from offering the child the help the Act envisaged.

Implicit in both these broad areas of criticism is the feeling among magistrates that they are no longer able to offer the general public the protection that it expects of the courts, against offenders of all ages. They also claim that recent statistics showing the startling proportion of all burglaries and violent crime committed by children under seventeen bears out their criticism. (In London, for instance, in 1972, 41 per cent of all burglaries and robberies were committed by children under seventeen.)

One magistrate explained,

> The young social worker, who to some of us looks no different from the children themselves, is often just not up to coping with difficult children. An aggressive boy from a difficult home just runs rings around them. It makes them and the court look foolish.

The force of this criticism can be judged from the not infrequent occasions when the bench remands a child to the care of a local authority and the child has not applied for, or has been refused, bail. In many cases, the magistrates allege, the child is allowed by the social worker concerned to go home, thus making nonsense of the bail refusal and increasing the risk of his committing yet further offences. Magistrates accept, however, that this may also be the result of the scarcity of secure places in which a child remanded by the juvenile bench can be kept.

A memorandum produced by the Magistrates' Association and sent to the Government in July 1972 sums up this fear.

When a juvenile appears before a court on an application for a remand without bail, justices are sometimes informed that the local authority cannot provide any secure accommodation. This may drive the court to the conclusion that a young person is too unruly for what the authority can offer and he is remanded to prison, which is most undesirable.

This power to commit a child under seventeen to prison or to a remand centre is given to the magistrates in section 23(2) of the 1969 Act, for those cases where a child is 'of so unruly a character that he cannot safely be committed to the care of a local authority'. In 1970 1,629 children under seventeen were in prisons and remand centres, and in 1971, the first year of the Act's operation, the number had risen dramatically – by almost 25 per cent to 2,040, which rose to 2,066 in 1972. The magistrates admit that this is clearly against the philosophy and spirit of the Act, but point out that they often feel they have no alternative in view of the persistent offences committed by a minority of offenders. They also accept that this is a strange result for a piece of legislation designed to remove children from the old-fashioned penal establishments.

This tendency on the part of the magistrates has also worried the remand centres themselves. Mr Philip Scott, Chairman of the Board of Visitors of Ashford Remand Centre, wrote to the *Magistrate* in June 1973, saying:

Ashford is intended for youths of seventeen to twenty-one years of age and has a very large catchment area, comprising the whole of the south-east of England. An analysis of the intake of boys under seventeen years classified as unruly was made for the month of September 1972 with the following rather disturbing results. The total number of young persons received under 'unruly certificates' was 138 and of these fifty-four had never been in care.

He goes on to give a breakdown of the 138 cases. Eighteen had been let out on bail but not yet sentenced. Fifty-four were sentenced to borstal, twelve to detention centres and one to a mental hospital. The remaining fifty-three boys did not receive any custodial sentence. Care orders were made for seventeen of them, supervision orders for nine, seven were fined and the rest, twenty boys, were conditionally discharged.

'These figures show that about 39 per cent of the young persons sent to Ashford as being too "unruly" to be committed to the care of the local authority had at no time been given the opportunity to behave acceptably whilst in care.' Mr Scott called on the local authorities to provide more secure accommodation for themselves and not rely on the Prison Service.

The Magistrates' Association memorandum stated also:

> Reports suggest that some courts may tend to by-pass care orders and make a detention centre order or a recommendation for borstal training, which, although not the first choice of treatment, is considered preferable to that available to, and offered by, local authorities. This is most undesirable and places an added strain on these overburdened institutions. Borstal receptions of younger boys have risen significantly.

The most recent official statistics show that in 1971 263 fifteen-year-olds and 741 sixteen-year-olds were sent to borstal. The comparable figures for 1972 were 278 fifteen-year-olds and 839 sixteen-year-olds.

These boys and girls also spend periods in either local prisons or remand centres before they appear for sentence at the Crown Court. They may spend a period of weeks or even months waiting for this appearance, and even then there is no certainty that borstal training will, in fact, be ordered. (In 1972 of more than 1,700 children aged between fifteen and seventeen committed for sentence to the Crown Court 995 were actually sentenced to borstal.) Some magistrates privately admit that they use their power to commit a child aged fifteen or sixteen for sentence to borstal at the Crown Court because they know he will spend a period in prison or remand centre before he appears there – even if he never receives borstal training.

As a result of the magistrates' misgivings about committing a child to the care of a local authority, they have increasingly tried to by-pass the care order for fourteen- to sixteen-year-olds, by sentencing them to a three-month period in one of the six junior detention centres. The pressure on these crowded institutions became so great that the magistrates specifically called on the Government urgently to provide more places, even though this was directly contrary to the stated intention of the 1969 Act. In November 1972 the Government accepted their argument and increased the number of places in the centres by 30 per cent, from 2,000 per year to 2,600 per year.

Many of the magistrates' criticisms centre around the character of the 'new breed' of social workers whom the 1969 Act suggested they rely on in its operation. They claim that these new social workers seem to be both young and inexperienced in dealing with troubled children. As one magistrate put it, 'How can these young people, fresh from university departments of sociology, but otherwise completely untrained and inexperienced, possibly understand the needs of a delinquent child from a deprived home in one of this city's slums?'

Magistrates are also perturbed that such a large proportion of the social workers now dealing with delinquents apparently not only know little about the functions and workings of the juvenile courts, but also appear to know very little indeed about the law which they are participating in carrying out.

They are also disturbed that many of these social workers are apparently hostile to the idea that the courts and the law should be concerned at all with children in trouble, whom they regard as needing social welfare and not the application of the criminal law. This has meant, the magistrates continue, that the fruitful co-operation that used to exist between the courts and the social services, particularly the probation service, has been seriously undermined, to the detriment of the children whom they are both trying to help. This again they see as being against the philosophy of the Act.

The magistrates also point out that where the social workers from the local authority are not directly involved in a case but are simply asked to provide reports on an individual child's background to help the bench decide the best course of action for that child, these reports are often incomplete – sometimes ignoring important aspects of a child's life – and inadequate. The reports demonstrate, the magistrates add, the failure of the social workers to understand and to co-operate in the functioning of the court.

9 'A Stopped Cheque?' Reactions from the Social Workers

Social workers accept that the reorganization of their departments that took place as a result of the implementation of the Seebohm reforms in January 1971 made it difficult for them to cope as well as they would have liked with the changes brought about at exactly the same time by the Children and Young Persons Act 1969.

They accept, for example, that the foundation of generic social work departments has meant that some social workers experienced in children have had to work in other fields as well. They also accept that sometimes those with different experience have suddenly found themselves confronted for the first time with difficult delinquent children and have been unable to cope. But they utterly reject the magistrates' implicit criticism that they are in any way 'soft' with the children under their care.

Mr Brian Roycroft, the Director of Social Services for Newcastle-upon-Tyne, has summarized the social workers' attitude in an article in the *Magistrate*, 'I believe we are getting a new breed of social workers with a tremendous commitment to their work and to reaching into the basic roots of social ills to cure them,' he said. He warned magistrates that they should not be

> misled into thinking that social workers see the soft answer to all problems and are always against authority in favour of the underdog. Social workers are not, as is often believed, against punishment. They are in favour of punishment for young offenders if it is a constructive part of a plan which will help the young person come to terms with himself and his surroundings.
>
> They are not against taking children away from their own homes if by doing so they stand a better chance of relieving tensions, of creating new and better relationships, and of helping the young person to learn about himself and his powers of self-control. Social workers are not in favour of young people committing offences and continuing to com-

mit offences in the community because this is not only wrong in itself, but pushes the young person further along the road of social isolation.

Mr Roycroft cited a survey carried out in the north-east of England during one quarter of 1972. In this period 271 children were committed to care, of whom only forty-three went home, a large proportion of them, he claimed, with the agreement of the magistrates.

The Social Work Service's first survey conducted for the Department of Health and Social Security in late 1971 and early 1972 stated that generally

> local authorities do not take the exceptional course of returning to their own homes children whom the court expected to be treated in a residential setting except on a considered view – based perhaps on further assessment or on a change of circumstances – that this is the best available course in the interests of care and control, or as a temporary measure pending further arrangements for residential care.

Directors of social services in the local authorities deny fiercely that the decision to allow a child to return to his own home, against the recommendation of the magistrates, is taken by inexperienced or ill-advised social workers. They point out that the whole concept of a generic social work department is that there should be a team of social workers, all of them having different skills and experience who could combine to consider particular cases together. They maintain that any important decision is only taken after discussion both with a social worker who has experience with children and with the individual social worker's administrative superiors.

The social workers feel that in general the magistrates exaggerate the numbers of children under seventeen who commit further offences while they are in their care. While they admit there are a number who fall into this category they point out firmly that the magistrates are in fact criticizing the 1969 Act itself. In the words of one social worker, 'Many justices, despite what they say in public, still do not really accept the philosophy behind the Act. They still bear a grudge for having some of their powers taken away from them.'

They also feel that many of the magistrates' criticisms are really governed by a failure properly to appreciate the role of a social worker and, particularly among the older juvenile magistrates, an antipathy towards the different style and approach of what has been called 'this marvellous and dedicated new breed of social worker'.

One younger social worker said,

Magistrates were used to having before them probation officers neatly dressed in suits and ties with short hair and a deferential approach. I am afraid that they are going to have to accept that young people with longer hair and wearing jeans can be, and are, competent to help the children in their care.

Even a justices' clerk admitted in an article in the *Justice of the Peace*,

Some juvenile court magistrates, resentful at what they feel is a diminution of their powers and bewildered at the confusion of approach in the way the Act has been implemented, find it easy to transmute their feelings into indignation at the real, or imagined, defects of social workers. When a well-known and trusted probation officer omits to provide a pre-trial inquiry report his lapse is regarded with tolerance, while a similar failure on the part of the social services department would be the subject of public censure.

The commission of further offences by a child in care of the local authority is regarded as a failure on the part of the authority, whereas the commission of offences in an approved school would formerly have been accepted as one of life's little tragedies.

There is considerable acceptance among social service departments that social workers are too often untrained – at present only approximately 50 per cent of the 11,000 have any professional training – but they point out that there are no resources to provide more training places. 'There are good young people knocking on the doors of places for training as social workers now,' Mr Kenneth Brill, general secretary of the British Association of Social Workers told us, 'but they cannot get a place.'

It is also true that social workers today have much more on their hands than ever before. The Seebohm reforms asked them to cope with a greater variety of human difficulties, including the disabled, the elderly, the mentally ill and children, and therefore increased the pressure upon them. But the number of social workers has not increased proportionately to the demands on their services.

Mention should also be made of a school of thought among some social workers that children who got into trouble had been offered too much help in the past.

> We must realize that in the past our children were better treated than any others in Europe, while now with the Seebohm reforms and the changed social workers they are simply being treated in the way the public would want them to be – as one of the many other demands on the time and facilities of the state.

There seems to be a considerable readiness on both sides of this debate to accuse the other of stereotyped reactions. Social workers for their part criticize the magistracy for putting too much emphasis on discipline and too little on love and care. They accuse them of being punitive, authoritarian and patronizing both in their attitude and the way in which they organize their courts.

'They often think that custodial treatment is the answer to almost any problem,' one social worker said.

> Very often they make their orders on a tariff basis, irrespective of the needs of the child. Before the Act, this meant that after trying conditional discharge, fining and probation for a young offender, almost automatically they sent a child to the approved schools, whether or not it was in any way suitable for his particular needs.

On a more subtle point, Mr John Burns, probably the most respected approved-school headmaster in the country, said, in March 1973, that courts have tended to assume that the 1969 Act suggested they give a child who committed an offence 'another chance'. But he went on to point out,

> It is more than doubtful that this application of the adult concept of justice has ever had much validity for socially deviant and maladjusted children and young people. This is simply because their ideas of justice are not those of society as a whole or that they are simply not comprehended by the children.

Addressing the Institute for the Study and Treatment of Delinquency, he added,

In addition to this there are other children who offend and continue to offend and reappear before the courts for the simple reason that what the courts regard as giving them another chance is for these children a question of being put back into the very situation with which they are unable to cope without help that is not forthcoming.

For their part the magistrates point out that in reality most juvenile panels, far from being old and reactionary, are made up from the younger and more liberal elements of the bench, although they admit the difficulty of recruiting suitably qualified younger people to the juvenile bench. 'Our job is to administer the law,' one magistrate said, 'and we must be seen to be independent in doing this. We also have to keep up the standards of justice and especially to see to it that the child's legal rights are not taken away from him by a social agency, however well intentioned, which is not answerable to anyone.' The magistrates also believe that one of the principal functions is to represent the views of society as a whole and to take these into account when deciding what to do with a particular child, and are resentful that their accumulated experience is being completely ignored.

It is important to emphasize that in many areas the magistrates and the social services departments co-operate successfully and have a mutual understanding and appreciation of each other's problems. In many areas, for instance, there are regular meetings between the two sides, where any differences of opinion there might be are fully discussed and a compromise reached. The Social Work Service's second survey noted an improvement in these relationships. Nevertheless, over the country as a whole there is too little liaison between the courts and the social services departments and too much unnecessary bitterness and distrust between them.

There is one issue, however, which completely unites both the courts and the social services departments – the shortage of accommodation of all kinds for the child who cannot adequately be treated in his or her own home. Criticism is also made of the existing institutions, and especially of the community homes which were formerly approved schools.

One of the prime causes of dissatisfaction on the part of the social services concerned an anomalous period between the coming into force of the 1969 Act in January 1971 and the complete assimilation of the approved schools into the community homes system. During this period headmasters at the more than ninety independently controlled approved schools were able to refuse to accept children whom the local authority wished to place in their care. There were cases of heads refusing particularly difficult children – those needing most help – even though the schools were often less than two-thirds full at the time. Although this anomaly has now been removed it has left a residue of resentment among the local authorities.

One of the most frequent criticisms of all the institutions for young offenders was and is that they placed too strong an emphasis on discipline and punishment. Many young social workers especially were imbued with the idea that the approved schools were virtually prisons for children. This demonstrates a profound misunderstanding of the schools. The events at Court Lees School in Surrey in 1967, however, did nothing to dispel the suspicion with which they were viewed.

Critics alleged that the staff of the approved schools tended to rely on discredited methods of dealing with delinquent children, and in particular that many staff were unable to form the relationships with the children which are now seen as such an important part of the process of rehabilitation. One possible explanation for this is that the schools have found it extremely difficult to recruit suitable residential workers, who have often come to them with little or no social work training and without any particular knowledge of children and adolescents.

A former children's officer has told us:

> Too many of the approved-school staff were recruited from those who merely wanted a place to live, those without sufficient education to get any other job, and the dedicated spinster type, who wanted the job in order to get the family she herself never had, but who was often not capable of controlling it once she had it.

The problem of getting good residential staff is unfortunately one which is still with us today, and indeed is getting worse.

Another principal criticism of the approved schools was that they were too often situated in inaccessible parts of the countryside, increasing the children's difficulty of keeping any real contact with their family, friends and society as a whole. 'These children are already isolated enough in their own minds, and to add geographical isolation as well is to compound their difficulties,' one social worker said.

The approved schools and the remand homes have also been hampered in their task by being housed in elderly buildings which were often not designed for that purpose. As interviews with children who have been to these schools show, their atmosphere had a profoundly depressing effect and this sapped the children's confidence in them as institutions which could help them. Children often came to regard the schools as mini-prisons. The staff too were often depressed by the apparent lack of concern for the physical conditions in which they and the children had to live and work.

One of the more telling criticisms of the approved schools and the remand homes was that they created a criminal subculture. Many of the boys sent to them were disruptive and sophisticated offenders, who, in a distressing number of cases, corrupted the other children – some of them non-offenders – who came into contact with them.

For their part the senior staff in the residential approved schools and remand homes feel strongly that they have come to be regarded as the Cinderella of the social services. They feel their contribution and experience in helping children has not been sufficiently understood and accepted and that indeed the schools have been treated as a dustbin for children no one knew what to do with. 'The social workers seem to think of us as some kind of inferior beings who know nothing about forming caring relationships with children and see themselves as being the only receptacles of all knowledge in these matters,' said a headmaster.

The approved schools fiercely reject suggestions that they are over-punitive or disciplinarian in their approach. It is accepted that some children in the schools are dealt with more firmly than others, but they claim this is for the positive reason that the staff have assessed the needs of the child and, using their experience, consider that he may respond better to a stricter régime.

Although the approved-school staff accept that they are often geographically isolated they argue that this is not their decision, but that ordinary members of the public will not tolerate them too close to their own homes.

The staff of the old approved schools reserved their most vehement comments, however, for the attitude of many local authority social service departments to the children which they have placed in their schools. The Social Work Service of the Department of Health and Social Security admitted in its first survey on the working of the Act that there were 'several instances of a local authority removing a child from a school, or promising him that he would be removed, without ascertaining the school's opinion of the child's needs'.

'How can we be expected to give the child the help he needs when we know that any moment the social worker may turn up and take him away?', one approved-school head asked. But, of course, children may leave the schools under their own steam. They may abscond. One of the continuing difficulties of the approved schools has been that children have run away from them. 'You can't love or help a boy if he's not there' is one phrase commonly used by staff.

This feeling led to a movement during the sixties to provide special secure units within the schools to retain those children who seemed most anxious to abscond. They were also to be used for the most difficult and disruptive children, who suffered from special personality problems. Since the three units now in existence were built they have almost always been full and unable to cater for the rising demand from the schools and local authorities they serve.

Of course absconsion is by no means a new phenomenon. Boys and girls have always absconded from the residential institutions, and have often committed offences while they were on the run. It is important to remember that children committing further offences while in residential care is not something which has been created by the 1969 Act. Nevertheless, it is giving rise to increasing concern and the Act offers no apparent solution to it. There are too few places where children who could benefit from some form of security can be kept.

There has also been a similar lack of secure places in the

remand system. Again this sometimes leads to the illogical and undesirable situation in which a particularly difficult child, for whom the local authority are anxious to find a secure place to keep him while they decide what help is best, cannot be found such a place because of the acute shortage.

While the approved schools, we believe, have often been unfairly criticized and over-maligned, it is fair to say that a minority of them have been consistently over-punitive, staffed by poorly motivated workers and have amply justified some of the attacks made on them.

Many of the criticisms listed are, of course, not the fault of the schools themselves. It is clear that for many years programmes for dealing with delinquent children in residential homes have been too low on the list of priorities of both local authorities and the Government.

The Act and the controversy surrounding it has thrown into sharp relief the past neglect in the whole area of coping with juvenile crime. The institutions have been the principal victims of the continuing neglect. Now, however, the Government is trying to improve the conditions in both the approved schools and the remand homes now that they are part of the community homes system. The twelve regional planning authorities created by the 1969 Act, for example, have prepared plans for the flexible development of all their residential institutions. Even so many fear that some regional plans will do little more than change the name plates on the outside of the existing institutions, thereby neglecting a prime opportunity to remedy the present shortcomings (although some local authorities will plainly grasp the opportunity to act as creatively as the 1969 Act envisaged).

Moreover, acceptance by the Government of even the best-intentioned regional plans does not necessarily mean that their programmes will be implemented. The purse strings are still held by the local authorities who will have to find the money to carry out the developments, and who will be subject to the same pressures as they face in respect of any other expenditure. Both local authorities and the Government are only too well aware that there has never been much political or electoral advantage in providing more help for delinquent children. Faced with the choice of building a community home or a new home for the elderly, few local authorities could withstand the pressure to do the latter. In any cutback in public spending, like the present one, facilities for delinquent children are among the first to suffer.

This relative lack of interest in the whole field has also shown itself in both central and local governments' failure to encourage sufficient expenditure on the training and recruitment of residential social workers. 'There is a crisis in residential social work now,' one deputy director of social services said. 'We cannot get adequate staff. There is no national attempt at co-ordinating either training or recruitment.' As a result some institutions, or wings of them, have had to be closed to young people simply because there have not been enough staff to man them. There is little point in constructing new buildings or expanding the number of residential places available if there is not an equivalent effort at the same time to recruit and properly train the staff who will serve in them.

The neglect shows itself too in the shortage of trained therapists and psychiatrists in the residential institutions. 'Some of our children who need a great deal of psychiatric help are not getting enough, while others who could benefit from a little are not getting any at all because of the shortage,' one member of staff of an approved school said. One reason for this is plainly not only that approved schools and remand homes pay professional psychiatrists comparatively badly for their work, but that they also have a comparatively poor reputation as institutions offering help to children, and do not attract much voluntary medical assistance. The same point applies to other forms of therapy.

The Government has also been criticized for not being active enough in pushing the regional planning authorities to produce their plans, and get them underway. More than three years since the Act's implementation only now are there beginning to be tangible signs of the regional plans – an essential part of the Act – having been put into effect.

The Government has admitted that there have been some major shortcomings. In July 1972, Mr Robert Carr and Sir Keith Joseph said, in a letter to the Magistrates' Association, that 'It is common ground that there are a number – apparently an increasing number – of difficult children and young people who cannot be contained in a system generally based, as the approved school system has been, on open conditions, home leave and so on.' They went on to say that an increase in the use of borstal for children under seventeen was undesirable, but offered little consolation.

'There can be no short-term solution,' they said, 'but we can look to the progressive development of special facilities for persistent absconders and difficult boys and girls in the regional systems of community homes.'

More than a year later, in October 1973, Sir Keith announced that the latest projection of future plans for secure places catered for 216 extra such places in 40 new short-term units, and a further 94 secure places in 14 long-stay units, by 1978. This assumed that all the regional plans would in fact be implemented.

Whilst these proposals were widely welcomed, there were still considerable reservations as to their sufficiency and whether they would in fact all be provided. Some experts felt that by the time the extra secure accommodation had been provided, the need for them would have increased substantially so that no real headway would have been made.

The suggestion has been made by more than one critic, that essentially the Conservative government was not particularly interested in this field. It had opposed many crucial parts of the Children and Young Persons Bill when it was in opposition, and then found itself having to put into force a measure with which it disagreed. Its decision not to implement some key sections of the Act was one illustration of its attitude. Its lack of urgency in implementing others was seen as a further demonstration of this.

An article in the *Justice of the Peace* sums up what has happened in these words:

> This measure was originally a Labour Bill which was bitterly opposed by the Conservatives in opposition who then had the task when in Government of putting it into effect. This they proceeded to do by the simple expedient of implementing only those parts of the Act with which they agreed. This in turn required extensive re-interpretation of the Act by way of statutory instrument so as to make some of its vital terms, such as 'child' and 'young person' stand on their head and bear

a meaning directly opposite to the normal . . . the resultant effect on the comprehensibility of this measure is quite staggering particularly for lay magistrates and social workers, neither of whom is expected to be a lawyer by training.

It can be strongly argued that many of the difficulties and criticisms that the 1969 Act has encountered would have been reduced had the Act been implemented in its entirety as it was originally envisaged. Its problems have, however, been exacerbated by the unhelpful attitudes adopted by some of the agencies responsible for its day-to-day working and misunderstandings between them, the Government's failure to act with any sense of urgency and to provide effective leadership and resources in an area which desperately needs them and the simultaneous major reorganization of local authority social services. The result has been that the laudable and far-sighted objectives of the Act have been contradicted by its practice, and the Act has tragically failed to overcome the neglect and apathy which has pervaded the entire field of juvenile crime for so many years.

10 Chronic Delinquency: Tidal Wave in a Sea of Naughtiness

It is easy to forget that children under seventeen account for an important proportion of the crimes committed in this country. Just how large an amount can be judged from the criminal statistics. In 1972, for example, more than 75,000 children committed 22 per cent of all the indictable offences in England and Wales. They accounted for nearly 40 per cent of all the burglaries and robberies and some 16 per cent of all the crimes of violence against the person. In some parts of the country these proportions are even higher.

In London Sir Robert Mark, the Metropolitan Police Commissioner, in his report for 1972, highlighted the role played by juveniles. 'There was a predictable growth in recorded crime, but the disproportionate increase in violent crime motivated by theft and the extent of the involvement of young people in it were disturbing,' he said. The figures in his report showed that 41 per cent of arrests for robbery were in respect of the under-seventeens.

The average burglar today, therefore, is much more likely to be a boy of sixteen who remains in the house he enters for less than a minute and steals a transistor radio, than the adult professional thief.

In the past, however, it has been all too common for politicians and administrators to forget the part played by juveniles in crime. They have accordingly concentrated almost all their reforming zeal on the adult criminal. It is only relatively recently that the juvenile's contribution to our country's crime has begun to be recognized as a major one. Even now only a small proportion of our society recognizes this fact. But realizing the magnitude of the problem is not sufficient. Action needs to be taken to fight it. Our contention is that the action taken has in no way measured up to the danger faced.

Magistrates assert that their courts are now confronting what is virtually a juvenile crime wave. They also believe, as we have argued elsewhere, that the Children and Young Persons Act 1969 has meant that they are powerless to act against it. That argument is partly rhetoric. The courts have confronted a substantial amount of juvenile crime for more than twenty years and have dealt with it more or less (mainly less) satisfactorily. They have in the past been hampered by a lack of institutions and by institutions which have been ineffective and out of date. Moreover, general lack of public interest in the problem of juvenile delinquency has meant that for many years there has been no public pressure on Government or local authorities for increased resources to improve the system.

But the way we treat juvenile offenders has also been hampered by a persistently idealistic approach. The child who comes before the court charged with an offence has come to be seen by some politicians and social welfare workers as simply demonstrating that he needs love, care and protection. That is almost certainly true. But, sadly, they then assumed that every child coming before the court needed only that and nothing else. That was a fundamental mistake. The working of the 1969 Act, which was based largely on the theory that children in court were showing their psychological, emotional or environmental deprivations and little else, has highlighted a group of offenders who might well be suffering from those deprivations but who need a great deal more than love and care.

It is apparent from our research and the discussions we have held that a vast number of offences are committed by a relatively small proportion of children. Most children who appear before the court never offend again. Many more have phases of 'naughty' behaviour in which they may appear in the courts on two or three occasions but usually only on trivial matters. This category does not on the whole constitute more than a minor irritation to society, and the children in that group grow out of it. There is then a category of offenders who may show some signs of real criminality, but mainly of a minor kind. Often from an inadequate home background, they can sometimes be helped without too much difficulty, even though this may mean their being taken away from home for a time. They are the children for whom the provisions on care, protection and control are really helpful.

But there remains a small group of children who are in continuous trouble, and who persistently commit offences. In the vast majority of cases they come from particularly deprived areas. Often there is mental or psychiatric disturbance as well. Another characteristic shared by many in this category is a desperately inadequate home and family life. They may well see crime as one of the principal ways in which they can express their own personalities, and their rebellion against society. These children are the ones who commit most of the serious offences, who show contempt for authority and the law, and who abscond from wherever they are sent. It is these children who are likely to grow up into the adult criminals of the future.

Our system is adequate to cope with the majority of children in trouble. It deals easily with the non-criminal child who has, uncharacteristically, committed an offence. It can deal too with the child passing through a delinquent phase of adolescence. But these children would in any case probably not offend seriously again, whether or not they appeared before a court, and whatever order the court made against them. The system also copes, although slightly more uneasily, with the child who shows criminal proclivities and needs to be supervised by, or placed in the care of, someone other than his – often inadequate – family.

But for the final category, the most dangerous one to society, the system is totally inadequate. It is this minority of children that the residential staff in the old approved schools and remand homes have been complaining about for years. 'There are some bad ones we cannot deal with. We never have been able to and the law has never been of any help,' sums up their attitude. The persistent offender and absconder, the really disturbed and difficult child – whether let off lightly or not – is consigned to a life of criminality.

The reason the law offers no help to this difficult and significant group of children is that it was never intended for them. The 1969 Act was designed very much with the average 'naughty' boy from an unhappy home in mind – the lad who might steal once or twice or drive away a motor car – but who would respond to a little love and care given to him by an experienced social worker.

The diagnosis for those children is optimistic. As local authority social services departments get over the teething troubles caused by their reorganization and by the redrawing of the map of local government in 1974 they will offer perhaps the finest form of social support and help to these children in the world. The Act for this majority of children will, we are convinced, prove a great success.

Unfortunately, it is not the majority of children in trouble who are our most serious and pressing problem, but the persistent offenders who are not responsive to the existing forms of treatment. It is they who will become the adult criminals, and it is they who will cost our society a great deal in crime and in prison costs in generations to come.

As Professor Winifred Cavenagh has so persuasively put it, in a memorandum on the working of the 1969 Act,

> One of the few well established criminological facts is that although the majority of juvenile first offenders do not appear before that or any other court again, the boy who acquires a *number* of convictions early is, on the other hand, a very bad risk indeed. It is therefore of the greatest importance that children should be prevented from adding to their criminal experience after the first finding of guilt if they are not to mature into hardened adult offenders.

It is our contention that the 1969 Act specifically allows a minority of difficult children to do exactly that. It does so because it has failed to provide the practitioners in the field with the right resources, institutions and expertise to help this specially important group of children in trouble. They are the ones towards whom the lion's share of the resources need to be directed, for they present us with the major potential cost. Yet our whole system of treating children in trouble lavishes the largest share of resources on precisely the children who are unlikely to become a real problem in the future.

For, as one very senior and experienced magistrates' clerk put it, 'The majority of children who get into trouble once never do so again. We should not be wasting our time with them. They could well be ignored by the law, they are no problem. It is the small minority we should be concentrating on.'

This 'small minority' was once described by Mr John Gittins, the former head of Aycliffe Approved School, in these words:

> They are a gross inconvenience to our existing machinery and they are nobody's direct responsibility. Nobody knows clearly what to do with them because nobody has adequately studied them as a group ... But the price we pay is that they disrupt the institutions through which they pass, they disrupt the community in their brief spells of freedom, and they themselves are usually unhappy and friendless.

Time and time again the complaint is, 'There is nowhere we can send that particularly difficult boy. We know we have to get him away from home but there is nowhere suitable he can go. We know he needs special psychiatric help or special training but there is nothing we can do. But if we allow him freedom he just commits more offences.'

It is this state of affairs that we are anxious to see ended. The children who are most in trouble are those who are difficult, who persistently offend, who do not blanch from physical violence and for whom the law offers neither realistic help, nor any deterrent.

If it is possible to isolate the kind of juvenile offender who causes most of the trouble to the courts and social services, it should surely be possible to devise some means of coping with him in a special way which would reconcile the two objectives of helping the child and protecting society more successfully than is being done at present.

The official criminal statistics tell us very little about the offenders. But what they show is that of the nearly 70,000 boys under seventeen found guilty of indictable offences in 1972, more than 4,400 of them had four or more findings of guilt made against them when they appeared before the juvenile court. This amounts to about 6 per cent. (Of the 6,837 girls under seventeen in this category 337 had four or more findings of guilt – about 5 per cent.) These figures do not include, of course, offences taken into consideration by the court at the hearing.

There is no recent estimate of the percentage of children under seventeen who might be called extremely difficult (in 1954 an estimate was made that 16 per cent of the boys coming to a classifying approved school suffered from single or combined defects of such severity as to make successful training unlikely).

We have had access to hundreds of case histories relating to children who have caused extreme difficulties. We have also held discussions with a large number of persons involved in dealing with children in trouble at every level.

As a purely working estimate we would like to venture that something in the order of 4 per cent of all the children under seventeen who appear before the courts on indictable offences in any single year may pose extreme difficulties. In bleak terms this could mean that more than 2,500 children would fall into this group, and, as we have explained, the majority of these are not receiving the help or treatment they need and society is not being offered any real protection from their delinquency.

How can we cope with these children? One obvious method, which has been the subject of considerable debate, is to provide more secure accommodation in which these children can be kept, while at the same time giving them intensive treatment to suit their needs.

At present there are about 170 secure places in the community homes system for the children who are violent, unruly or disruptive and need to be kept in one place. There are also twelve secure places in the one existing youth treatment centre for specially disturbed children. If all the secure places announced by Sir Keith Joseph in January 1973 are built according to plan there should be by 1978 about 730 completely secure places for children under seventeen outside the prison system.

At present the shortage of secure accommodation means that difficult, especially violent, children in trouble are all too often being sent to prisons or remand centres designed for offenders over seventeen. In 1970 (before the 1969 Act came into force) there were about 1,600 children in the prisons and remand centres. But in 1971 the figure had risen to more than 2,000 and it remained at about that level in 1972. If the aim is to offer humane and caring treatment to children in trouble the persistent or difficult child offender deserves it more than almost any other. But he is not likely to receive it in the prisons or remand centres.

There is an urgent need for secure accommodation with adequate trained staff to help these children within the community homes system. It is a tragedy that they have been ignored for so long. We are not suggesting that every child who gets into serious or persistent trouble needs to be kept in secure conditions. What we are saying is that it is essential, both for society and for the sake of some of the children themselves, that they be offered a reasonable chance of getting the help and treatment they so badly need. We believe that this can often best be given to them in conditions of security. What form this security should take will be discussed later.

Those children who will not commit offences again will never need secure places, and those who are temporarily disturbed at home will continue to receive the help of social workers, but the minority of children who present the biggest problems to our society and to the existing system for dealing with delinquency will, we believe, under the system we propose, be coped with sensibly and effectively for the first time. If we can help the most persistent and the most disturbed offenders as children by an adequate system of courts and institutions the benefits to society will be incalculable, and might go a substantial way towards cutting down adult crime.

As a corollary to our thesis that much more attention should be paid to children at this extreme of the criminal spectrum, we also suggest that, at the other extreme, the trivial offender can be dealt with more often than at present without bringing him to court at all. The role of the police in this respect is crucial.

Whether he is caught riding his bicycle on the pavement, stealing from the local supermarket or driving away someone else's car, a child's first contact with the law is likely to be with a policeman. The police have a central role to play in the way children in trouble are treated. The traditional view of their responsibility – based on nineteenth century puritanism – was that a child who did something wrong deserved to be punished. The police, therefore, were seen as part of the process of punishment.

But as the emphasis of legislation on children in trouble changed to a more liberal approach, so did the attitude of police officers as well as the Home Office and the police authorities who are responsible for them. The principle that children in trouble might need help as much as punishment gained ground among the police.

The first official expression of this change of heart came in 1951 with the foundation of the Juvenile Liaison scheme in Liverpool. This was clearly based on the philosophy that the best way to cope with juvenile delinquency was to identify potential delinquency before it became actual and then to take preventive action. Each police division in the city of Liverpool appointed a specially chosen liaison officer who was charged with the task of preventing juvenile crime. These officers had nothing to do with the officer who may have caught a child doing something wrong. They took an interest both in the children who had committed offences, in cases where it had been decided to caution rather than take to court, as well as in children who had committed no offence at all but were felt to be potential delinquents. They identified these children, for instance, by discovering them keeping 'bad company' or playing truant persistently.

The liaison officers visited parents in problem families, as well as youth clubs and schools (which are regarded as one of the best settings for identifying potential delinquency). They acted in many ways exactly like social workers, taking advantage of their local knowledge and status in the community.

A number of other police authorities subsequently adopted schemes of a similar nature. The decision as to whether or not to set up a scheme lies entirely with the Chief Constable and is not the responsibility of any government department.

In London, which inevitably has the lion's share of delinquency, the Metropolitan Police did not formally try to prevent delinquency developing but instituted instead the juvenile bureaux in each of their divisions. As described in an earlier chapter, officers of the Juvenile Bureaux are not responsible for visiting children who have not committed an offence, but they do maintain close liaison with the local authority social services departments and education authorities about the records of particular children.

Juvenile Bureaux are common to most police authorities in the country. Through them the police are able to decide which children should be prosecuted and which should not. There are no fixed criteria governing the exercise by the chief inspector of the bureau of his discretion whether or not to prosecute, although he will clearly pay attention to the recommendations of his officers. This system means, however, that there are variations in the police practice about cautioning children who get into trouble from area to area.

In a survey in 1972, the *Sunday Mirror* showed that whether or not a child offender was taken to court by the police tended to depend on where he lived. In Teesside, for example, only 11 per cent of children were not taken to court. At the other extreme 74 per cent of the children in Devon and Cornwall who came into contact with the police were not taken before the court. Variations between the big cities, however, is not so wide. In the conurbations, between 40 and 50 per cent of children who come to the police's attention for committing offences are brought to court.

Nevertheless, there is little doubt that large variations in cautioning practice undermine the law and make it difficult for the general public to understand the system for dealing with children in trouble. The difference between the regions can mean, for example, that a child might be prosecuted for stealing a bottle of milk in Kingston-upon-Hull but might not be taken to court at all for threatening an old lady with a knife in Plymouth.

Deciding not to take a child to court does not mean, of course, that he gets off without any form of reprimand. Every police force uses the power of the official caution for those offenders it does not bring to court. As described earlier this means that a child is given a formal warning by a uniformed police officer, and is told that if he commits any further offences he is almost certain to land up in court.

The variety of attitudes among police forces as to whether to take an offending child under seventeen to court or to caution him is a fundamental weakness in the system for coping with children in trouble. The courts should not have to deal with children who have committed only minor offences, and are obviously unlikely to do anything naughty again. This wastes the court's time, the taxpayer's money and police effort. If an official remedy is needed at all for such minor cases a caution is clearly the correct approach. The magistrates themselves have been constantly annoyed in the past by having to deal with boys and girls who have committed only trifling offences and with whom the police could have dealt with perfectly adequately.

There is a clear need for one consistent pattern of police action in coping with children. This both gives the public confidence that something is being done about delinquency and at the same time prevents the law from falling into disrepute, through being seen to apply the judicial sledgehammer of the court on very small nuts indeed.

The Home Office should co-operate with the police authorities in England and Wales to produce a uniform code to advise chief constables which offences and offenders should be brought before the court and which should not. This would clearly not be a binding code, but it should act as an authoritative guide and be disregarded only in exceptional circumstances. Sensible guidelines should inhibit police officers from bringing merely naughty children to court for minor offences. For, as has been said, many children go through a period of naughtiness at some time in their lives and a court finding of guilty, however trivial the offence or small the penalty, brings with it a criminal record which may unfairly act to the child's disadvantage in later life.

As the vast majority of children who brush with the law will not do so again once their adolescence is passed and as they are not persistent offenders and present no long-term difficulty to society, they should not be treated by the police – even implicitly – in the same way as adult offenders. Indeed it would matter little if their crimes were completely ignored. It would save the time of the police and the courts and the efforts of social workers without imperilling society in any way.

In a previous chapter we pointed out the ambiguous role played by the police when they visited the homes of children who have committed offences in an effort to help in the decision on whether to caution them or take them to court. The possible conflict between the law enforcement and the social welfare roles of the police officer have obvious dangers, some of which might be avoided if the caution were to be used more often.

If there were sufficient local authority social workers, it would be far better for them to prepare the reports on a child's home background for submission to the police before the decision to bring before the court, to caution, or to take no action was made. This would, however, place an even greater strain on these already overstretched services, and it would be unrealistic and facile to suggest this as a solution.

Is it better then to have no home inquiry about a child in trouble or to continue the present system of using the police to do it at this stage? The juvenile bureau system appears to be fulfilling a real need in helping children and no major conflicts of the kind that are described here appear to have arisen or, rather, have become publicly known.

In these circumstances, therefore, and because we believe it is essential to have as full an investigation as possible before a child is brought to court, there appears to be no practical alternative to allowing the police to carry on with these home visits. It is essential to warn the police that this is a difficult role for them to play in their attempts to help children, and one which would be better fulfilled by a social worker.

With the help of Home Office guidance as to what offences or types of offenders merited a warning, an official caution or a court appearance, and the establishment of juvenile bureaux in every force to help this decision to be reached, we believe the police could continue to perform a vital function in helping children in trouble.

Individual officers themselves, however, must realize that they cannot use the weight of the law simply to take a child to court for any offence. The interests of justice might sometimes be far better served by their turning a blind, or at least, an only mildly cautionary eye to many of the smaller incidents in the lives of children. If the police can do this it will free the magistrates for the more urgent task of dealing with those children who present a major difficulty to society.

11 Cash, Compassion and Containment

Before turning to the specific proposals which we made to reform some aspects of the role of the juvenile court it is important to explain briefly why we believe that the court should be retained at all in dealing with child offenders. There have been numerous criticisms of the courts' role and of the magistrates who sit in them. In most cases the critics have reached the conclusion that the court should have nothing at all to do with children.

For instance, both *The Child, the Family and the Young Offender* in 1965 and the Kilbrandon Report in 1964, relating to Scotland, recommended that the juvenile courts should be abolished altogether. In Scotland this has now been done and a system of relatively informal children's panels substituted. This appears to be working well. Most other European countries, too, do not use criminal courts for children. Why then retain the juvenile courts, with their many faults, for England and Wales?

Our view that it would be best to retain these courts is not based on the comparative study of the strengths or weakness of the English and foreign systems. It is mainly founded on the purely practical point that any move to abolish the juvenile courts altogether – whatever substitute for them is envisaged – would have absolutely no chance of being accepted by the Government (whichever party was in power) or of legislation to that effect being passed by Parliament. Nor would such a move correspond with the wishes of the vast majority of the public.

It is generally felt that decisions which may dramatically affect a person's future should be surrounded by as many safeguards as possible. The law provides one such safeguard. Children have legal rights, just as adults have, and these need to be protected and seen to be protected. The public, rightly, has an abhorrence of decisions apparently taken in secret. The fact of a child making a public appearance and being seen to be dealt with according to the law by an independent body of people instils confidence that his rights are being safeguarded. On the other hand, decisions taken, however well motivated, in the private rooms of a local authority office, or anywhere else from which the public or its representatives are excluded, are open to considerable suspicion.

Juvenile court magistrates are open to attack on many grounds. But the system is not, we believe, so beyond redemption as to warrant its total jettison. We therefore prefer to make practical proposals to reform the court and the role of juvenile magistrates so as to meet many of the objections made against them rather than, unrealistically, to call for their abolition.

If it is accepted, as we have argued, that the main problem lies with a relatively small proportion of children, some way has to be found of separating these and dealing with them in a different manner from that used for the vast majority. In simple terms the difference is between the naughty child and the persistent or disturbed delinquent. At present, the same system tries to take care of both and is unsuccessful with the really difficult child.

The juvenile courts have been part of this system and have been equally guilty of concentrating too much effort on the 'naughty' children. Our proposal is for a two-tier system in the courts which will make a formal separation between the two categories of children, and allow the difficult cases to be given additional attention and more resources.

This separation would be made by the ordinary juvenile court magistrates before whom the child appears. The magistrates would have before them (as they do now) social inquiry and other reports on the child's family history, home circumstances, environment and attitudes. It will also have his record of previous appearances before the court. On that information they would be required to make an assessment as to whether the child before them presents a sufficiently difficult problem to warrant his being classified as being persistent or particularly difficult.

The decision would be made by the magistrates partly on the basis of how often the child has appeared before the court in the past, partly on the number of offences he has committed and their nature, and partly on the contents of the reports before them.

In our view, if a child comes before the court on three separate occasions within a period of, say, six months he should *prima facie* be considered as being a persistent offender, except where the nature of the offences is so trivial that the magistrates decide otherwise. The magistrates could also use their discretion to declare an offender persistent, even if he has appeared only twice, or his appearances are spread over more than six months, where the number of offences he has committed (those with which he has been charged added to those which he admits and which have been taken into account) exceeds a certain number, say, twenty-five. The magistrates should always retain some room for choice, and the test should always be: does the child's conduct show a persistent course of serious delinquent behaviour?

Once the magistrates decide that the child belongs to the category of persistent offenders the case would then be remitted to a special panel of magistrates who would give more detailed consideration to it. They would have the help of the social and medical agencies and would have a greater range of powers at their disposal than the ordinary member of the juvenile court bench.

The special panel dealing with a particular case would consist of three magistrates with special knowledge or wide experience of juvenile delinquency. Theoretically, of course, all magistrates appointed to the juvenile bench are supposed to be 'specially qualified' to deal with children. In practice, however, this is no more than a formula that means little more than that the person in question likes children and thinks he or she understands their problems – a supposition which is demonstrably untrue in many cases. The proposed members of the special panels would have to prove their special knowledge. This requirement could be satisfied by academic qualifications in, say, criminology or sociology, or by previous professional qualifications (a significant number of magistrates have, for instance, social work qualifications), or by experience of direct involvement in juvenile crime, including, of course, long service as a juvenile magistrate.

The power of appointment to the special panels from the existing body of juvenile magistrates would be vested in the Lord Chancellor. He would make the appointment only after he had been shown to his satisfaction that the applicant (whether nominated by an advisory committee or putting forward his own name) had the necessary qualities for the panel. The additional administrative burden involved in bringing this extra tier in the juvenile courts into operation would be minimal as it is unlikely that more than 200 magistrates, spread around the country, would be needed to sit on the special panels.

The three special magistrates dealing with a case would receive all the papers which were before the magistrates who first dealt with it, in addition to the short reasons as to why the child had been classified as persistent. The panel would then be able to call on the knowledge and experience of the social worker involved, or a probation officer who knew the family, or the director of social services, or on any relevant doctor or psychiatrist, for whatever elucidation they might need. This could either be done before the child was due to come before them or, in particularly difficult cases, it might be thought necessary to have the social worker or psychiatrist present at the hearing.

The panel hearing itself would be more informal than the original court appearance. It would be, preferably, in a different office, and only the child, his parents or guardian, the magistrates and their clerk, and the welfare or medical representatives would be entitled to be present.

Panel magistrates would have more powers to deal with the offender than the ordinary juvenile court magistrates. It is, of course, possible that in some cases the panel might feel that the child should not have been declared a persistent offender in the first place, or that a lenient approach was appropriate. In that case they could deal with him by the usual methods of fine, absolute or conditional discharge, supervision, detention centre, attendance centre, or placing him into the care of the local authority.

Where, however, the panel felt that something more needed to be done, the magistrates should have the power to send the child to an institution themselves and not have to rely on the local authority to make that decision.

It is true that prior to the 1969 Act there had been complaints about magistrates' misuse of their power to send a child to an approved school. But these had arisen largely through magistrates not understanding what the approved schools were meant for, and what kind of children should be sent there. The result was that the approved schools became a receptacle for offenders in respect of whom the magistrates had no real idea what else to do. Magistrates also sent children to the approved schools merely because it was the next stage in the 'tariff' of the penalties available to them, irrespective of the needs of the children. Often very little thought went into the making of an approved school order and there was insufficient contact and trust between magistrates and the social agencies involved.

Our proposals are admittedly designed to put important decisions into the hands of magistrates, but only those who have the knowledge and understanding to make them, and who have the best and fullest possible advice. In a growing climate of trust between the various groups who deal with juvenile crime there need be no reluctance to give these extra powers to the magistrates.

Their powers to send a child directly to an institution would apply not only to baldly stating that the child should be placed in a community home, but also to stating the kind of home required. For instance, they might specify, where necessary, that he should be kept in a secure unit or be sent to a place where a particular kind of treatment was available.

We believe that this system would provide sufficient safeguards for the rights of the child. Appeals would continue to be made from the magistrates' decision to the Crown Court and in addition there could be incorporated into the system a review of the panel's decisions by the Department of Health and Social Security. If necessary, there could also be a regular six-monthly review of individual cases by that department.

In addition to the new powers we have proposed, much could be done to improve the ambience of the court hearing to the benefit of the child. There is no valid reason why the procedures and the language of a juvenile court case should not be made more informal without necessarily taking anything away from the authority, dignity and effectiveness of the law and the magistracy.

Magistrates and lawyers are rightly concerned that the child's legal rights should not be taken away from him and say that it is essential in order to safeguard these rights to have proper legal procedure, especially in contested cases. Accepting this, it should nevertheless be remembered that the vast majority of offences are not contested. It should therefore not be necessary to conduct the proceedings in the atmosphere of a trial.

There appears to be no logical reason, for instance, why there should be a uniformed policeman in the court (as is the practice in many juvenile courts) or why the child should be questioned in a formal, legalistic manner reminiscent of an adult trial when he could obviously tell his story much better in his own words, or why everyone concerned should always have to stand when giving evidence or making a statement or answering a question.

Many social workers feel strongly that they are prevented by the magistrates and by the procedure from making a real contribution to the interests of the child because of the way in which magistrates often insist on the old formal relationship during the case, which effectively does not allow the social worker to say anything unless invited to do so by the bench. Too often magistrates appear to forget that what is important is the social worker's relationship with the child. They should, perhaps, be reminded more often that they are not holding 'mini-trials'. Apart from the procedures much more can and should be done to ensure that juvenile cases are not dealt with in what in so many instances is only a slightly modified courtroom structure.

All the suggestions we have made would be rendered of no value, however, if the institutions to which the persistent and difficult child offenders were sent were not able to give them the care and treatment which is the object of sending them there in the first place.

The provision of secure residential institutions should be a principal tool in the machinery for helping children in trouble. At their best such institutions can provide better care and understanding for a disturbed child, or a persistent offender, than any social worker trying to make the most of a poor home environment. It is surely preferable that a disturbed boy be sent away to a reasonable residential home where he will receive adequate treatment than to be offered help in the poverty and degradation that is often the hallmark of the only place he knows as home. The argument in favour of carefully organized regionally based residential institutions, providing some measure of security, is, we believe, unanswerable. They can provide the difficult child with the security in which he can best receive the therapy or training which he may need. The security need not be of an Alcatraz or Parkhurst type. All that is needed is good perimeter security. Within the institution the atmosphere should be that of freedom.

This is not to punish the child in any way, for with adequate perimeter security the institutions themselves can provide a number of different régimes depending on the kind of children in whom they happen to be specializing. They could, for instance, offer training for apprenticeship, as many of the approved schools do, or they could place more emphasis on psychiatric therapy.

It is envisaged that children would remain in the secure institutions for not less than eighteen months. No child will be able to leave them simply at the request of his or her social worker. The headmaster or headmistress of the institution involved would have the right to appeal against any application for a child's release before a period of eighteen months was up, and the Secretary of State for Health and Social Security – whom we feel should be the judge of any appeals against release – would ordinarily not release a child unless the case for doing so was overwhelming. It is obvious that for a specially difficult child to respond to the kind of environment that we have in mind for these institutions he or she must have a prolonged period there in which to begin to reap the benefit. The perimeter security of the institution is of paramount importance. Within the perimeter, however, we believe that the régime should not in any way be punitive or repressive. There is no contradiction between security and a caring humane environment. Sadly there has been a contradiction between the two in the Prison Service – and even more tragically in the special hospitals for the criminally and often violently insane – but there is no reason for there to be this in the institutions envisaged. These should be specifically designed, or adapted, for children under the age of seventeen taking into account that they should not be allowed to leave them at will.

One model for these institutions does in fact exist, in the adult prison system – Grendon Underwood. This prison was established by the Prisons Department to cater for specially disturbed prisoners who were believed capable of responding to treatment and for whom a good chance of rehabilitation was thought to exist. For those children who have demonstrated particularly disruptive tendencies, for example, the model of Grendon Underwood might well be a useful one for the community homes to keep in mind.

The Department of Health and Social Security's three youth treatment centres (of which only one is in operation) are obviously influenced by this example. But even when the three centres are completed – at the earliest in 1975 – they will not be able to cope with more than a total of 140 boys and girls. We believe that this is not enough secure provision for very disturbed children.

At the other end of the spectrum there may be other children who would benefit from security, but who would need very little psychiatric treatment. For these children the emphasis in our secure institutions would be on training for possible future employment and on social education to help them understand and integrate with the society which they will be rejoining. This must be training based on the child's needs and interests and not on the random availability of staff to teach a particular trade or skill.

It is of paramount importance to repeat again that these secure institutions should not be seen as 'para-prisons', nor should they be considered as being punitive. We do not advocate the locking up of children in cells (indeed the fewer locked doors and rooms within the institutions the better) and there should not be the emphasis on discipline and the military approach on which the existing secure institutions so often seem to rely. The staff of these institutions should never, in any sense, be thought of as warders. They would be there as social workers, counsellors and advisers in exactly the same way as they would in other closed communities – such as those for the mentally disturbed.

The quality of the staff, therefore, is of prime importance, for however adequate the buildings and other facilities, it is the staff's contribution that will be the crucial factor in the success or otherwise of these institutions. They will have the responsibility for helping children who have, in almost every case, been neglected throughout their lives by their families and by society. In our view the staff of residential homes for children should be specially selected and more highly paid than the equivalent non-residential social workers. It should be recognized financially that they are in the front line of helping children in trouble. Staff in residential institutions, and particularly in the secure ones, not only need a special dedication to their task. They also need special training and qualifications for it. Too often in the past residential social workers in the approved schools have been poorly paid and have suffered from poor working conditions. Because of this residential posts in the institutions have been difficult to fill with suitably trained, interested, and motivated applicants.

Of course, not every community home would need to be secure. Indeed, the great majority would not be. But additional security measures should be provided for on a contingency basis at a number of homes in case of a need for it. One of the great weaknesses of the institutions helping children in trouble in the past has been their inflexibility. Too often there have simply not been enough secure places, nor enough remand places, nor enough places in which children could be classified, and it has been impossible to convert what facilities existed to these uses.

Taking remand first, it seems clear that there will be an increase in the amount of remand accommodation available to the courts once the twelve regional plans for the community homes are implemented. This is to be welcomed. It also seems likely that other community homes will be adapted to provide more places to remand children under seventeen. This is essential, for at present there is a severe shortage of remand places, which often forces the local authority and its social workers to allow the child to return home, when it might be better for him, and prevent him from committing further offences, if he were kept in a secure remand home.

Mr Brian Rycroft, the director of social services for Newcastle-upon-Tyne, remarked in *The Magistrate* of June 1973: 'Every regional plan includes more provision for assessment centres and every local authority in the country has accepted the need to develop these expensive and unpopular establishments.' He went on,

> The availability of remand home places has been short for a long time and the implementation of this Act did not immediately make any difference. I know it is true that we are often taking longer to assess children and I think we are doing this for the right reasons and therefore the remand homes and assessment centres are taking fewer children.

A secure observation and assessment centre place will not necessarily mean the child will go on to our proposed more secure institutions. Indeed he or she may only spend time at the assessment centre before being called before our proposed special panel of juvenile magistrates, who might then decide that he or she would be best served by going straight back home.

One difficult problem is that of where to place children under seventeen who are remanded to the Crown Court with a recommendation that they be sentenced to borstal. It seems incredible that magistrates and local authorities are still prepared to tolerate the present situation in which children are often remanded in adult prisons before being sent up for sentence or until a borstal place is found for them.

Clearly if there were more security available in the community-home system then the magistrates could remand to those institutions instead. Conditions for children in adult prisons are admitted by all to be unacceptable. It is a ridiculous commentary on legislation that was supposed to remove children from prison and punitive conditions that the numbers spending periods of sometimes months in these establishments should still be rising (there were more than 2,000 under seventeen in prisons and remand centres in 1972). This situation provides another strong argument in favour of more secure places in the community homes, run by people with experience of children, and not by staff who normally would be manning prisons.

Outside the community homes system we see no reason why the attendance centres should not continue. While the positive value of a régime which seems to consist mainly of press-ups or basket-weaving is doubtful, the fact is that attendance at the centres at least keeps some violent football hooligans off the terraces and some vandals temporarily off the streets on Saturdays. It may even in the very exceptional cases act as a deterrent to some potential delinquents. Moreover they fulfil a certain public relations role in that they appear to be accepted by the public as a useful tool. Attendance centres, however, can have absolutely no effect on the disturbed and difficult child, and cannot be expected to cope with the children in our category of difficult or persistent offenders.

Detention centres, too, could well be retained for a period under the system we envisage. Since the implementation of the 1969 Act the magistrates have come to use these institutions as a 'dustbin' for every persistent offender whom they were no longer prepared simply to remit again to the care of the local authority. In consequence they rapidly became full and considerable pressure built up on the Government to expand the number of places in them, particularly for children aged fourteen and fifteen. (In January 1973, Sir Keith Joseph announced that a further 600 or more junior detention centre places annually would be made available because of this pressure.) The theory that magistrates (not necessarily those on our special panels) should be able to send children who have committed offences to the detention centres seems to us to be defensible in the short term. The brief period of rigorous training they provide, coupled with security, can in some – but only some – cases, which need to be carefully chosen, be a possible antidote to delinquency. The development of the community homes, however, should mean that the emphasis on detention centres will progressively decline, as envisaged by the 1969 Act.

Borstals, on the other hand, seem to be entirely unproductive and unhelpful for children under seventeen. These institutions are unhappily being used by the magistracy to deal with children who persistently commit offences and for whom the detention centre and the care order have provided no help.

The pressure on places at the borstals has risen so fiercely over the past decade that they are really no longer capable (with a few exceptions) of offering the training which was one of their objectives when they were originally founded and which they managed to carry out so successfully during the thirties. They have all too often descended into being merely the first step on the road to prison, and their residents realize that that is what they are. Again, if the community homes system fulfils its potential it should obviate the need to send children under seventeen to borstal at all.

Of course there will always be extraordinary cases for which the system of institutions we have suggested will not provide. But we would hope that the scheme of combining treatment and therapy with security in the more difficult cases would give the general public more confidence in the law and the system for treating children in trouble. It would also render less virulent public appeals for lengthy periods of more traditional custodial treatment for children whose offences are particularly violent or anti-social. And it would also – and this is obviously the most important result – help the children.

But all the improvements we have suggested cannot alone deal with the problem. What is also required is more goodwill and understanding between the various agencies involved in dealing with the delinquent child. Up to now there has been a significant lack of trust between the courts and the social services, which has severely undermined the work which both of them should have been trying to do. Happily, there has recently been more liaison between these two groups. In some areas it could fairly be said that there is now complete co-operation and mutual understanding. But in others the old suspicions linger and in some cases there has been an almost total breakdown in contact.

Equally, there has also been mutual misunderstanding between the residential staff of the old approved schools and the local authority social workers. What is clearly needed is much better and fuller liaison and exchange of information and views between the police, the courts, the social services and the institutions, with the interests of the children themselves always kept firmly in mind. Whether this liaison is done formally by means of a committee, or informally, matters little. What is crucial is that each party has trust and confidence in the ability and objectives of the others when they are dealing with delinquent children.

In the short term the proposals that we have made will lead to some increase in direct expenditure on trying to cope with children in trouble. But in the longer term, and taking into account savings in other areas, we are convinced that implementation of our ideas will not result in any additional expenditure, and may, indeed, save money.

If, for example, more care is taken to see that children are prosecuted only where there is no other way of dealing with them, there will be a saving in the time spent by the police in bringing a child to court and presenting the case against him.

Equally, as far as the juvenile courts themselves are concerned, at the first stage, fewer children coming before the court will mean that the magistrates should have more time to sit in the adult magistrates' courts, or would be able to spend a greater proportion of their time on the essential task of looking into the background and cases of the individual child offenders. On the new special panels we believe that the time spent by members in dealing with a persistently offending child need not necessarily be excessive. In any event, there is not at present that much pressure on many of the juvenile magistracy to cause any grave concern about finding the time for these special panel sittings. There should certainly be no need to recruit more magistrates. Nor should there be any need for extra accommodation to be found in the courts themselves.

Resources are still desperately needed, however, for the building of all kinds of new institutions as well as new juvenile courts, some of which are still in extremely old premises, their gloomy atmosphere continuing to reflect the punitive approach to children in trouble. However sympathetic the magistrates, such surroundings are almost certain to be counter-productive. Some of the former approved schools and remand homes, too, are in Victorian buildings originally designed for completely different purposes. As we have pointed out, the effect of conditions like these on both children and staff is considerable and long lasting.

It is, of course, difficult to press the needs of juvenile offenders over those of old-age pensioners or the disabled or mental patients. There is still an attitude of 'throwing good money after bad' in this field. But what is often not appreciated is that unless children in trouble are dealt with adequately and with understanding at an early stage they will not only continue to offend as children, and be a menace to the society around them, but are also likely to turn into the adult offenders of the future. They will then be a far greater menace to society, and it will then cost far more to deal with them whether in or out of prison.

On buildings, however, although present resources are inadequate, the additional expenditure need not be intimidatingly large. As it is, the twelve regional planning committees' plans will provide for a number of new residential homes as well as for the adaptation of existing ones. Provided that these plans are implemented and imagination is used in building as wide and flexible a range of homes as possible, these plans should in most respects prove reasonably adequate to meet the physical need for places. The only area in which they will not be adequate is in the provision of security where necessary. For even if all the proposed secure places announced by Sir Keith Joseph are built they will amount to a total of only about 580 in the entire community-home system, plus some 150 in the youth treatment centres.

As we have explained we believe that there may be a need for as many as 2,500 more or less secure places in the community homes and the youth treatment centres. This need not necessarily mean adding to the regional plans. It is possible to provide in advance for the conversion of ordinary accommodation into secure accommodation when the need arises. As for the youth treatment centres calling for exceptional resources because of the extremely difficult cases which have to be coped with in them, these should continue to be the direct responsibility of the central government, as they are at present, and not be a burden on local authority funds.

On the social services side our scheme would mean a re-allocation of resources rather than an increase in expenditure. The various officials involved in dealing with children at present would continue to do so. But there should be a dual saving. The local authority social workers should have fewer children committed to their care by the courts. They would also have to spend a smaller proportion of their time on the persistent offender, whom we envisage would be likely to be taken into the hands of the institutions. As a result the social workers would be able to offer an improved service to the majority of offenders placed in their care. They would also be able to provide better information for the courts and the proposed special panels of magistrates than they would have time to do at present. A further advantage might also be that they would be able to spend more time and effort in offering help and advice to the families of the children in their care, or in the institutions.

The biggest problem, however, is likely to be finding an adequate number of high quality residential staff rather than in raising money or building new premises. There is already a crisis in the residential care service. There are too few well-qualified and trained staff to man the existing institutions. The reasons for this is not only poor pay and conditions. It also is the reluctance shown by many suitably qualified people to live at the institutions in which they work, thereby sacrificing their privacy and leisure and rendering a normal social life impossible. There is a clear case for launching a full inquiry into ways of introducing the 'shift' system as much as possible into residential homes. A shift system is already being applied, to some extent, at the St Charles Youth Treatment Centre at Brentwood. But by the very nature of the treatment required by the children in these institutions 'shift' work cannot be a complete solution to the residential staffing crisis. Difficult children need to form relationships, and this cannot be limited to particular times of the day.

A sharp increase in funds available for the recruitment and training of residential social workers is of prime importance if we are to offer any sort of real help to the children who need it most.

Our society must reconcile itself to the idea that it is going to lock more children up in the future than in the recent past. We believe this is the only possible way to help deal with the growing problem of juvenile crime and to help the juvenile criminals themselves. We do not come to this conclusion lightly, nor do we do so for the traditional reason of wishing to see the wrongdoer punished or deterred, but because we believe that residential institutions may offer these children, and therefore in the long run society as a whole, the best possible hope for their future.